OWN
YOUR CAREER
OWN YOUR
LIFE

STOP DRIFTING
AND TAKE CONTROL
OF YOUR FUTURE

ANDY STORCH

ISBN Paperback: 978-1-7360209-1-3

ISBN ebook: 978-1-7360209-2-0

Book Design by Maria A. Rodriguez

Cover Design by Vanessa Mendozzi

Praise for Own Your Career Own Your Life

"The happiest, most engaged employees are those who take active ownership of their career and success. In *Own Your Career Own Your Life*, Andy Storch has written a wonderful guidebook to help you take ownership of your career and command of your life. This book is a must read — no matter what stage you are in your career."

Marshall Goldsmith, New York Times #1 bestselling author of *Triggers, Mojo*, and *What Got You Here Won't Get You There*

"*Own Your Career Own Your Life* is an incredible reference manual for every person who wants to design a life they are truly proud and joyful to live! With stories that will engage you and make the book impossible to put down, resources that will become a part of your daily life, and ideas that will spur you on to a more successful life and career, this is the very next book you need to read! Get your copy and carve out some time to read it right away!"

Honorée Corder, Strategic Book Coach, Author, *You Must Write a Book*

"Andy Storch is such an inspiration in the way he is constantly learning, networking and taking action for growth. In *Own Your Career Own Your Life*, Andy shares stories and practical wisdom and lays out exactly how to set a vision and go out and achieve your goals both in your career and your life. This book is all about taking ownership and having the right mindset and preparation to tackle anything in your career and life and I'm honored to be mentioned."

Hal Elrod, international keynote speaker and best-selling author of *The Miracle Morning* and *The Miracle Equation*

"Andy Storch has written a masterpiece with *Own Your Career Own Your Life*—explaining exactly how you should go about taking ownership of your career and life and take control of your future. If you are looking for a way to jumpstart your career, look no further. This book provides inspiration and practical advice to shift gears and achieve your goals including all the right habits to adopt all the way."

Garry Ridge, Chairman and CEO of WD-40

"Whenever I tell people about Andy Storch, I describe him as the 'sunniest' person I know. In life, it's rare to meet someone who sets clear intentions for their life – and acts upon them to set their dreams into motion and create the reality they want. Andy does that – and in this book, shares how you can stop drifting and start taking control of your career so that you can truly start to embrace life and enjoy it in all of its technicolour glory. If you're looking for a book with strategy, written by someone who has taken their own advice (and made it work!) with a dose of humility, humour and heart? Then this is the one for you."

Jessica Lorimer, Founder of Selling to Corporate and author of *Smart Leaders Sell*

"Reading *Own Your Career Own Your Life* is like sitting down with Andy and getting a master course in living your best life. Drawing upon his own experience and examples from others, Andy offers readers the concrete guidance as well as kind (yet persistent) challenges to make the changes required for greater success. If you're ready to trade old habits for new, more productive ones, this book is for you."

Julie Winkle Giulioni, Author of *Help Them Grow or Watch Them Go*

"The best employees are those who feel confident, passionate and fulfilled in their work and where they are going. In *Own Your Career Own Your Life*, Andy Storch has written a guidebook that every employee should read to take ownership of their career and more control of their future."

Susan Schmitt, Chief HR Officer, Applied Materials

"I've learned that it doesn't matter how good you are at what you do. If you want to ensure your future success, you've got to take ownership of your career and do the important things like building a network and a personal brand. Nobody is better than Andy Storch and I'm so excited that he's sharing all of his wisdom and advice in this book. If you follow the advice he lays out in this book, you are guaranteed to have a happier and more successful career (and life)!"

Rachel Richards, Bestselling Author of *Money Honey*

"Andy provides practical wisdom for the "new normal" and so succinctly defines the critical features required to drive an autonomous career. He draws upon his own personal and often humorous experiences to paint a compelling view of career navigation ignited by passion, that keeps you not only relevant, but well-networked, and prepared for the future of work."

Kelley Steven-Waiss, Founder & CEO, keynote speaker, futurist and author of *The Inside Gig: How Sharing Untapped Talent Across Boundaries Unleashes Organizational Capacity*

"Andy's not writing from some ivory tower. He's walking the path, and picking up wisdom and scars and blisters and insights along the way. This book shares the journey, and helps you set a plan for your own career."

Michael Bungay Stanier, author of the WSJ bestseller *The Coaching Habit*

"If you want to go fast, go alone, but if you want to go far, go together." is an apt sentiment cited in this fantastic book, *Own Your Career, Own Your Life*. With a light-hearted, mentor-next-door vibe, Andy successfully distills larger than life concepts into actionable steps that you can take today. His practical approach brings into focus a path forward with relatable examples that normalize life's ups and while unleashing the passions that you never before dared to explore. In the age of awakening, the timing for this powerful message is now. Whether you are a seasoned professional or in early career, this must-read book offers life-changing guidance on intentionally realizing the vision for your life and career with a timeless framework that can be applied through every phase of your journey. The perfect addition to any reading list, I strongly encourage you to get your copy today."

Adri Maisonet-Morales, Vice President of Enterprise Learning & Development and Blue University for Blue Cross Blue Shield of North Carolina

"In *Own Your Career, Own Your Life*, Storch offers practical and applicable content that applies to anyone looking to grow personally and professionally. He authentically offers his own experiences as an action-taker achieving big goals, and yet, he also recognizes that taking ownership may look different for each individual. The easy-to-read style paired with the simple-to-implement 'old habit vs. new habit' sections makes this book one that each reader will walk away with added value to their career and life."

Renee Vidor, author of *Measuring UP: How to WIN in a World of Comparison*

"Our lives and our work have always demanded integration. *Own Your Career, Own Your Life* is a masterclass that will empower readers in myriad ways: from crafting a vision to connecting with purpose to building a personal brand

and so much more. This book is a must have for seasoned professionals as well as those just getting started."

Mike Flynn, Entrepreneur and #1 Amazon Best Selling Author of *Master The Key: A Story to Free Your Potential, Find Meaning* and *Live Life On Purpose.*

"We live and work in unprecedented times with work changing drastically and so much uncertainty about the future. *Own Your Career Own Your Life* provides a clear blueprint for how to set a vision, make a plan, get intentional with your actions and prepare for the future of work and truly own your career. No matter where you are in your career, you can benefit from the lessons in this book and establishing some of the great habits Andy recommends. This is a must for everyone."

Lindsey Pollak, New York Times Best Selling Author of *Recalculating: Navigate Your Career Through the Changing World of Work*

"As someone who is dedicated to serving others and making the world a better place, I love what Andy has done with *Own Your Career Own Your Life* as I think it truly has the power to inspire millions of people to stop drifting and take ownership of their careers."

Claude Silver, Chief Heart Officer at VaynerMedia

"In *Own Your Career Own Your Life*, Andy Storch leads the way into this new world that we are racing into. Storch does a masterful job of blending practical advice, real life wisdom, and an inspiring vision on how you can take ownership of your career and your life. I have been fortunate to have a front row seat as Andy has authentically used his passions to not only build a personal brand and a powerful network for himself, but to watch him help so many others do this for themselves. There has never been a more important time to take ownership of your career and Andy will be your expert guide to lead you to an incredibly bright future!"

Vincent Pugliese, Owner of Total Life Freedom and Author of *Freelance to Freedom*

"Reading *Own Your Career Own Your Life* is like having a personal conversation with Andy Storch over a cup of coffee. Through sharing his personal career journey, he teaches readers how they too can take the reigns of their career and live the life they've always dreamed of. It's not difficult to feel a spark being lit for your own career as Andy shares tangible examples of how his tips and advice have driven his own career success."

Christine DiDonato, Author of *Get There Faster: The no-nonsense, no-fluff guide to the career you want*

"I've watched Andy Storch for years and been amazed at how he's re-imagined his career, networked with industry A-listers, and manifested his dreams. Now, he reveals how he's done it—and how you can too—in *Own Your Career Own Your Life*. This is a must-read book whether you're a recent college grad or are mid-career and want to change professions."

Kevin Kruse, Founder of LEADx and New York Times bestselling author of *Great Leaders Have No Rules, 15 Secrets Successful People Know About Time Management,* and *Employee Engagement 2.0*

"Andy Storch delivers a narrative and informative career development book for workers at all levels. With actionable items, sage advice and a very conversational tone, Storch achieves an easy-to-read manual for how to develop career focus and achieve success (whatever shape that looks like for you) with ease."

Lisa Spinelli, editor of *Teachers to Trainers* and ATD Senior Content Manager

BEFORE YOU START READING

Thank you for picking up this book. I wrote it to help you take ownership of your career, life, and future. There is a lot of valuable information and advice in this book, but it will be worthless if you don't write things down and put them into action.

To that end, I highly recommend keeping a journal nearby or using the notes app on your phone. If you don't have a journal, I have a list of recommended journals you can try using in the free resources section on my website. I have also created a companion journal to this book that you can use to write down thoughts and track progress toward your goals. Search for the Own Your Career Own Your Life Journal, and you'll be on your way. Using a journal has been an incredibly valuable resource to me over the years, and I know it can be for you as well.

In addition to writing things down, you need to share, get accountability, and help. If you want to get even more value, encourage a friend or colleague to read this book and do the activities along with you.

Finally, because I didn't want to cram too much into one book, I have created several free resources to help you with some of the activities. We also have a free community on Facebook you can join, where you can connect with other readers and people who are taking control of their future just like you.

Head over to ownyourcareerownyourlife.com and get everything you need.

And be sure to follow me on social media as well:

LinkedIn: https://www.linkedin.com/in/andystorch/

Instagram: @andy_storch

Thanks! Enjoy the book! And don't forget to take action on everything you learn, and tell me what you did!

DEDICATION

To my wife, Cortney and our kids, Lucy and Teddy. You give me purpose.

To my parents who raised me to love books. I've been reading books my whole life and now I've written one too!

To my mentors and friends who have pushed and inspired me to never stop challenging myself and striving to achieve my goals.

To life, which is so mysterious, challenging, wonderful, and whatever we make of it.

TABLE OF CONTENTS

INTRODUCTION

Most careers happen accidentally. Someone recommends a major or a course in college or a trade school, and we choose it because we don't have any better ideas (that's what I did). Or we take a job for money (or desperation) and several years later find ourselves in that same field without ever really being intentional about what we are doing (that happened to me).

And there's nothing wrong with starting a career that way. We all have to start somewhere. And very few people are born knowing exactly what they want to do with their life. Even if they do, they often face unexpected challenges and have to make changes. Without a clear vision or goal or a plan to achieve that goal, most people drift along, mostly reacting to life. I have been there myself many times.

When I was growing up in Orlando, Florida in the 1980s, my dream was to be a professional baseball player. I was a huge Chicago Cubs fan, and my favorite player was second baseman, Ryne Sandberg. It's odd to think back to my childhood and remember I had multiple posters of a grown man on my wall. I knew nothing about him other than his baseball stats, and yet he was my hero and exactly who I wanted to be. He was cool, calm, and consistent. And my dream was to one day play professional baseball, ideally for the Cubs.

And there is nothing wrong with a dream like that. Many kids have them.

But there were multiple challenges to me ever achieving this dream. The first, of course, is that the odds of becoming a Major League Baseball player were (and still are) incredibly small. A quick internet search tells me a Little League Baseball player has about a 0.03% chance of making it to the "Bigs." That's one out of ever 3,300 kids who play baseball.

The second problem was that I wasn't that good. I played consistently from ages six to fourteen, and I had some successes over the years. I really enjoyed it. But to be honest, I was never really an "all-star" even in the mediocre, suburban little league I played in.

Maybe the biggest problem and the one that anyone trying to achieve big goals can relate to and learn from was that I never really had a clear goal or plan. Nor did I put in the extra effort needed to make it to the next level.

I was just practicing when the coach said to practice and playing in the games, hoping to get better. But I never sat down with my parents or coaches and said, "I want to make the pros one day. How can I get there?"

Because I didn't have a clear plan, I never got the extra help or coaching I needed, nor did I spend enough time trying to improve the things I needed to improve. I had a very "fixed mindset" (more on that later) about sports and life and was always afraid of making mistakes. As a result, after playing baseball for many years, I gave up on my dream at fifteen. I didn't even try out for my high school baseball team because I knew I wouldn't make it. And just like that, my baseball career ended.

The same thing happened to me in college. When I arrived at the University of Florida as a freshman in the Fall of 1998, I was pretty certain that I wanted to be a civil engineer. I have always been enamored by roads and tracks and bridges and transportation and thought it would be pretty cool to design them. After some investigation, I found out that is what civil engineers do and chose it as my major. I had done well in calculus and physics in high school and felt confident I would achieve this dream.

But then I got to college, joined a fraternity, started spending a lot of time socializing and drinking and not enough time studying. Oh, and then I ran into chemistry class. It was a bad combination.

I excelled in math and physics (the main subjects needed for civil engineering), but chemistry did not come as naturally to me. And because I didn't study enough or ask for help, I decided I just wasn't good at chemistry (hello fixed mindset), and, eventually, I dropped it and was forced to change my major.

Looking back, it seems sad and ridiculous that I couldn't pass that one class, but it is part of my journey, and I think it still serves as a good lesson today. How?

Because we will always encounter challenges in life, and unless we have a strong vision and purpose and drive to achieve a certain goal, those challenges will likely knock us down. I wasn't intentional about what I was trying to achieve or how I was going to get there. I had a general idea of what I wanted to do (graduate and be a civil engineer), but I didn't think too much about it. And I certainly didn't put that purpose or goal above the fun things like going to parties with friends. Can you relate to this? Has this been you in the past?

I was drifting and having fun and living in the moment, which is not uncommon or bad. But by being reactive and not having a clear plan or being intentional about where I wanted to go with my career and how I wanted to get there, it set me back many years. I chose a new major reactively because it seemed easy, and I heard it would lead to a good-paying job. But I did not pursue it seriously. I didn't do anything to enhance my chances of getting a good job after graduation. With the US facing a mild recession when I graduated in 2002, I settled for the only decent job I could find—in a manager training program at Walgreens.

That job was unfulfilling, and I left after a few months to try some other things that didn't work out either. After my girlfriend (now wife), Cortney, graduated, we moved across the country to California, and I tried several other jobs and startups before getting an MBA. Even with the MBA, I still had no idea what I wanted to do and ended up in a job I disliked for a few years until I lucked into a consulting job that turned things around for me at thirty-one.

That job led to me learning many of my strengths, finding mentors and friends, and eventually rediscovering my desire to become an entrepreneur, using my powers to help others.

I tried many things and had many frustrating moments and luckily my wife, Cortney, stuck with me through it all.

Today, I run my own business, host two podcasts, run a conference and membership community, and have a great marriage and kids. I love my life. I'm doing work I enjoy with a mission that invigorates me, and I have a huge network of supportive friends and colleagues. But it took a lot of mistakes and hard work to get here. Now, I'm on a mission to help others do the same and live life more intentionally. Because no matter what stage of life or career you're in, you can always make changes and benefit from being more intentional with your life and career. And that's what this book is about.

This book is about taking control and owning your career and life. It's about achieving your goals. And it's about taking control of your future.

I started by sharing a couple of examples of how I was drifting and not being intentional with my own life and how that resulted in me failing at my goals. I have some other stories I'll share later. I've made a lot of mistakes (haven't we all?). And having a big network and lots of conversations has shown me that I'm not alone.

Like everyone, I've had plenty of successes and failures, but I was never truly satisfied until I took more ownership and control of my life and career. And now I'm happier and more fulfilled than ever.

I'm not perfect. I still make mistakes and have tons of room for improvement. But I am working on it every day. I'm learning from every success and mistake, and I'm trying to find ways to improve all the time because my mission is to fulfill my true potential and inspire others to do the same.

Who Am I and Why Am I Writing This Book?

Before we get started, you might be wondering who I am and why I wrote this book.

I will start by telling you my purpose, which is to love and support my family, continuously grow and improve, model a healthy and intentional lifestyle, and change the world by inspiring people (like you) to live more intentionally and love their lives like I love mine.

My name is Andy Storch, and I consider it my mission to fulfill my true potential and inspire others to do the same. I get so inspired and excited by helping and inspiring others.

How am I doing that? Let me count the ways. First and foremost, I'm a husband and father. I'm also a consultant, coach, speaker, facilitator, podcaster, conference host, author (yay!), and friend to so many.

I have an MBA, a large network, experience doing a lot of different jobs (most of them not so great), have started multiple businesses, traveled to over thirty countries, facilitated business workshops for thousands of people around the world, attended a ton of conferences (I get asked about this a lot) and made a lot of great friends all over the world (I'm especially proud of this). My wife, Cortney, and two children give me love and purpose and are an important part of my mission.

In 2016, I got into personal development and started living more intentionally after reading a book called *The Miracle Morning* by Hal Elrod. At the time, I had a life that looked successful on paper. I had a six-figure consulting job, was married with a daughter and another child on the way, and plenty of friends. But something was missing, and I didn't quite know what it was.

The Miracle Morning sent me on a trajectory of self-discovery, learning, trying new things, changing my career, becoming an entrepreneur, building a personal brand, improving my marriage, starting podcasts, and many other things.

Hal's message and book changed my life, and now I want to do that for others.

That's a big reason for this book. Not only do I want to help others learn from some of the big changes that I made, but I have also interviewed and worked with hundreds of business leaders and talent development leaders from large companies. I have heard stories of high turnover and employees not truly taking ownership of their careers. I know there is a better way, and that's where this book comes in.

The idea for this book came to me like a lightning bolt while I was having a conversation with a friend at a conference in London. Two months later, I was writing it. And now, I'm excited to have it published and in your hands.

Now let's get started!

PART I

Own Your Career

Why you need to stop drifting and take control

What does it mean to own your career?

The way we approach and think about careers has changed quite a bit since I started working and even more since my parents and grandparents started their careers.

From the Industrial Revolution to the late 20th century, it was pretty normal and even expected that most people would choose a career (and even one company) and stick with it from high school or college until retirement around age sixty-five.

My grandfather and my parents were public school educators who started teaching after college and all retired around age sixty with a pension and full retirement plan. That used to be normal for many people but is changing quickly.

When I graduated from college in 2002, I think it was accepted that people might move around every five to ten years and have two to three different employers or careers. People worried about their image and what employers might think if they moved any more than that. If you left a job after less than three years, it might look bad on your resume!

As I write this in 2020, the old rules don't apply much. It has become quite normal for people to move around and try different things. Sometimes, they even go out on their own and try consulting or entrepreneurship and then go back to working for a company. Many people, especially millennials, want to explore, find their "passion," try working on their own and for others, and see what suits them best or supports their purpose.

Things have changed a lot over the years, and employees are less loyal to their employers, and their employers are less loyal to their employees as well. As a result, people have more freedom and move around a lot more.

It is easier than ever to look for a new job if you are unhappy with the one you have. All you have to do is jump on LinkedIn or any job site or reach out to friends to ask about their companies. I've even heard of companies promoting jobs and hiring via Snapchat and Instagram.

But I don't think that means employees are better off. Many of them are searching for new jobs without giving their current job, employer, or career a fair shot. They never took the time to think about what they truly wanted and then communicated it to their manager and colleagues. They are often drifting and being reactive. Similarly, I've read that online dating and apps like Tinder cause people to give up on relationships quicker and go searching for a new one (I have been married since long before Tinder existed, so I have no experience with this). It's so easy to look for a new job; I wonder if people give up on their jobs too early to search for a new one.

That's why it becomes more critical to own your career. But what does that mean?

Own Your Career – The Definition

For this book, when I say, "own your career" or "own your life," that means taking full responsibility and being intentional with your actions. It means having an idea of where you want to go, making a plan, and then taking steps to get there. It means that you don't wait for others to tell you what to do or where to go. It means you don't blame others for your problems. Yes, there will be things that happen outside of your control, but owning your career means you focus most of your energy on what's in your control and keep moving forward.

You can think of it as owning a business. When you are the owner of a company, no matter what happens in the world or economy, you are responsible for everything.

Owning your career also means doing what you can to prepare for the future so that when crazy things happen (like the COVID-19 global pandemic), you are better equipped to respond.

Besides global pandemics, the business world is changing all the time. The pace of change is faster than it has ever been and is getting faster all the time. Companies are getting disrupted, and jobs are changing, and things are probably not going to settle down anytime soon. So, the clearer and more intentional you are with your plan and actions, the more prepared you'll be for the future.

The future of work is always uncertain. But I can say with confidence that many of the jobs that exist today (no matter when you are reading this), likely won't exist ten years from now and that there will be tons of jobs and businesses created in the next decade that were not even imaginable today.

For example, I'm writing this book in 2020, and Social Media Manager is a very legitimate job title and career that is probably done by thousands of people for different companies. Just about every major company probably has a team of people that strategize, listen, and react to things on social media. Even authors and entrepreneurs, like me, seek help with this. I hired a friend just to run social media for my conference and will probably do the same for this book. That would seem silly ten years ago and didn't exist at all fifteen or more years ago.

Perhaps the biggest reason to take ownership of your career is simply that nobody cares more about it than you do.

Seriously, your parents and significant other and even your friends might be rooting for you and supporting you. And if you're lucky, you might have a great manager or mentor who gives you guidance, coaching, and advice. But nobody, and I mean nobody, cares as much about your career as you do!

So, you can sit around waiting for others to tell you what to do, or you can start taking ownership, getting intentional, and blazing your own trail. I would rather own my career and life because I've learned that other people don't care as much about my career as I do. They have their own lives to worry about.

That's why I want you to start thinking more about your vision, purpose, and goals and how you'll achieve them. Taking time to figure those things out is rare in our society but comes with many benefits.

How often do people truly have a vision or know their purpose? How often are people willing to sit down and have that conversation with their manager or colleagues or function leader? I don't think it happens enough. We are going to change that.

In this section, I will outline the steps that I think every employee (and entrepreneurs too) should take to have more ownership of their careers. That includes setting a vision, connecting to a purpose, making a plan and setting goals, taking responsibility, asking for help, and having productive conversations.

CHAPTER ONE

SET A VISION

Do you know where you are going with your career? A lot of people don't. But you would probably never get into your car or on a plane or even start walking unless you had an intended destination and knew exactly where you wanted to go. I bet for most of the smaller actions in your life, you have a goal or plan in mind. But for our careers, we often have no idea.

And that's okay. I'm not here to preach to you that you must have a vision for your career. Early in their careers, many people have no idea what they want to do. But can you imagine how much better things would be if you did have a vision or goal? Because with an intended destination, you can start making a plan and having more confidence in your decisions and actions. And the cool thing about having that vision and plan is that nothing is ever set in stone. Unless you are signing a contract to join the military or law firm as a partner, you can almost always change your mind later.

I have personally changed my vision and goals many times. Early in my career, I thought my big goal was to be a successful company executive or CEO of a big company one day. Then, I started to dabble in entrepreneurship and thought maybe I could start a company and make a lot of money. When that didn't work, I got an MBA and started searching for a career that would make me happy.

Then I decided that as long as I was making enough money to get by and enjoy my life, that was all I needed. Except it wasn't. I realized I wanted more. I wanted to run my own business. So, I left the consulting company to become an independent consultant and started chasing money and freedom.

Along the way, I realized I had the potential to make a significant impact on the world with my message, and I changed my vision and goal to something bigger.

As you can see, I'm a bad example of how to plan your career and, simultaneously, a great example of how we can always change our minds and pivot in our careers. For many years, I was so unsure of myself and where I wanted to go. I didn't know myself or what I was capable of, which made it harder for others to help me.

As a result, I drifted for many years, and I didn't have a real plan until recently. But you can. And you can start right now.

Things will change over time, and challenges and opportunities will come along, but the more we have clarity for where we are going, the easier it is to make a plan and have confidence in the moves we are making.

What Should my Vision Be?

When you are ready to set your vision and make a plan, it's important to first remove any pressure. You are not being graded or judged, and you can always change your mind. Your vision does not need to be grand. Some people may set a goal or vision to one day be CEO or a partner in their firm, while others may say they just want to enjoy their job and work reasonable hours so they can spend more time with their family. There is no wrong answer. The key is to have something written down so you know where you're going (or trying to go).

Let's say you currently work in marketing, but your dream is to work in sales or HR. You probably aren't going to get there unless you declare it to yourself and start making a plan.

This vision can look as far out as twenty years down the line or as close as one or two years. It does not have to be concrete. The point is to have an idea of where you want to go with your career and then use that to guide your decisions.

A Vision Can Help Guide You

While not everyone has clarity on where they want to go or what they want to be when they grow up, it can be helpful. The biggest reason to have a vision or plan is that it helps guide important career decisions. Depending on how long you've been working, you have probably already experienced a few of these critical decisions. For example:

- Your company or boss offers you a promotion or a new job doing something different than what you're doing now

- Your boss tells you that you are not meeting expectations and won't be getting the promotion you wanted

- A friend invites you to come interview for a job at his or her company
- A recruiter reaches out to you about a job you are qualified for
- Your spouse or significant other gets a job offer in a new city
- You have children or health issues that cause you to reconsider how much you are working
- You have one too many bad days at the office and decide you want to make a change
- There is a leadership change in your company, and your priorities or job description changes and becomes different from what you signed up for or are used to.

All of these things are real situations that happen weekly all over the world. Most of them have happened to me in my career. Any time one occurs, how you respond will have a big impact on the rest of your career.

Most people don't have any vision, plan, purpose, or values to help guide their decision and just go with their gut (or more likely, what their boss or friends recommend). I know because I have been in a couple of these situations.

Let's look at an example of something that happens often.

Jennifer works in finance for a large corporation and has been doing well lately. She exceeds all expectations and gets along great with the team. Her boss comes to her one day and suggests she's in line for a promotion to a director role that will provide her with more money and authority, but she will have to put in more hours at the office to learn the role and get everything done.

Many people accept this promotion because they want the money or status or just feel like it's the right thing to do. Maybe they don't want to disappoint their boss or company. Besides, everybody wants to move up and make more money, right?

But what if Jennifer's dream is to work in HR or Marketing. She loves people and making an impact or wants to learn more about marketing and thinks it would be a lot more fun. Or maybe Jennifer likes finance, but she is really into fitness and family, and the long hours would potentially prevent her from spending time doing the things she loves. Would accepting this promotion still make sense?

There is no right or wrong decision here. It comes down to personal values and preferences. But knowing our values and having a vision can help us make the best decision. And we can always pivot and change later if things don't work out. But accepting that promotion and starting that new job as a director of finance would certainly make it harder to make that shift to HR or Marketing later. If Jennifer is trying to grow a side business as a personal trainer or spend more time with family, this decision could cause stress as well. That's why it's so important to tap into personal values and vision to inform these decisions.

If Jennifer has spent time reflecting on her strengths and desires and where she wants to go in her career, and knows she wants to try moving to HR or Marketing, she could use this as an opportunity to have a real conversation with her boss. She could say something like, "I am so grateful for this opportunity, and I'm sure it would be valuable for my career, but I have discovered I really love working with people and have been thinking about trying to get into HR or Marketing. I'm wondering if we can make a plan for me to do that instead."

Now every company and situation is different, and I don't know how open Jennifer's manager would be to this conversation. Still, the point is that Jennifer has a vision for what she wants to do and is taking ownership of her career by starting this conversation instead of just accepting whatever comes her way (as most people do). Sharing her goals with her manager will make it much easier for her manager to help her achieve her career goals.

You can see that without a vision or plan, Jennifer probably accepts this promotion or blindly accepts advice from her boss or colleagues. But with a vision and plan, she can pause and decide if it fits so she can make a more informed decision.

I have plenty of examples from my career, where I had opportunities come my way. Sometimes, I didn't have a vision and had no idea what to do. On other occasions, I did, and the answer came easily. Recently, a very successful and popular thought leader in the HR space reached out to me to offer what seemed like a pretty lucrative business opportunity to work with him.

I was flattered and honored that he had thought of me and felt compelled to at least consider it. But after giving it just a little bit of thought and talking with my wife and another good friend, I realized that accepting his offer would require a major shift in what I'm doing and a detour or departure from my vision for my career and life.

As a result, I took less than forty-eight hours to consider it and then sent him an email to politely decline (while leaving the door open for future opportunities and partnerships).

Had I not had a clear vision of where I wanted to go, I might've agonized for days about this and then second-guessed myself no matter which option I chose.

I don't think there is ever a right or wrong decision in these situations, but having a clear vision of where I want to go made it much easier for me to make the decision.

A Vision Can Give Peace of Mind

Things can, and will, change (more on that in a moment), but until they do, it's nice to know where you are going. I read once that tranquility and peace are often found in identifying our path and sticking to it *(Daily Stoic)*. That means knowing where you want to go, staying the course, making adjustments as needed, but not getting distracted by living a life suggested or demanded by other people.

As in my example above, having a clear vision makes it easier for me to evaluate opportunities when they come my way. And I can promise you that the more successful, experienced, and connected you become (especially if you follow my advice in this book), the more opportunities will come your way. And if you're like me and have a hard time saying "no" or making big decisions, then having that clear vision of where you want to go will give you peace of mind and make those decisions so much easier.

Things Change

As I mentioned previously, nothing is set in stone, and things can change. Maybe Jennifer gets what she wants and moves to HR, and after a year or two working there, she decides that it's not what she thought it would be and wants to move back to finance. Or maybe she gets bored and wants to try marketing or sales or start her own business. Maybe she has children and decides to be a stay-at-home-mom. There is nothing wrong with any of these things as long as she's intentional with her decisions.

Some say the only constant in life is change. We know that the economy will change, your company will probably change leadership at some point, jobs will be eliminated or created, and your situation will change as well. The days of accepting a job at twenty-two and working in that role or function for thirty-five years until retirement are over. Studies show that most people will have at least seven to nine job or career changes in their lives. So, don't worry about things changing. Just because you decide at twenty-five that you want to be company CEO one day does not mean you have to keep pursuing that goal five years later when you have kids and decide you'd rather spend more time with them.

The other thing about time is that it provides more clarity and wisdom. Time does not necessarily make people smarter or better looking, but it usually brings wisdom, which means that with more experience, you can make more informed decisions. And I can tell you from my own experience that at twenty-five, I had no idea what I wanted to do with my life or career. But at forty, I have a lot more clarity and know exactly what I want to do.

And even that might change. Because at forty I know I'm still just getting started and twenty years from now, I might be doing something completely different. That's okay.

The world and your life will continue to change, and I want you to be ready for it. That means setting a vision but remaining flexible and being prepared for change.

How to Set Your Vision

Setting your vision does not need to be scientific or a long process. It just involves you pausing or reflecting on what you want to do or who you want to be. That means setting aside time with a pen and notebook and no distractions, and writing down what you enjoy about your current job or career and all the things you don't like. Then write down the things that might be missing from your career that you might want. After that, write down some jobs (if any) that are attractive or intriguing to you that you might like to try.

In her book *Get There Faster*, my good friend Christine DiDonato says it's important to start by discovering your energizers and values. Your energizers are the things that you love doing. They give you more energy instead of draining your energy. I get energy from being around people and love giving presentations, facilitating, and getting on calls. You might be the opposite and love doing quiet, analytical work. We are all different and get energized by different things.

Similarly, it's important to know your values. Your values are the things that you believe are most important in the way you live and work. I've done this exercise a few times, and it's always difficult to prioritize but can give you a lot more clarity on what's most important to you.

If you do a quick Google search, you'll see plenty of free exercises to help you determine your top values. The way it usually works is you look at a list of 100 or so values and narrow it down to the values most important to you and then keep eliminating them until you arrive at your top five most important values.

It's a very difficult exercise because you'll want to say all the values are important, but the point is to decide what's the *most* important, which helps you make decisions in life. For instance, health and relationships are both important, but when the chips are down, and you have to choose between happy hour or the gym, which one will you choose?

Another book I recommend that can be helpful with this process is *Designing Your Life* by Bill Burnett and Dave Evans from Stanford Design School. This book walks through the process of design thinking to figure out what you want to do with your life or career and design it in a more fulfilling and meaningful way. Burnett and Evans teach readers top "think like a designer" principles when designing their lives and careers, and this process can help decide where you want to go.

Once you've gone through this process and written down your likes, dislikes, pros, cons, and potential career options or big goals, it can help get feedback. Talk with your family and friends who know you best and ask them some questions. For example:

Where do they see you going?

What potential do they see in you?

What ideas do they have for you?

What things do you do better than anyone else they know?

Remember that while it can always be helpful to seek guidance and advice from family and friends, you are not obligated to follow it. Just because your mother says you should become a lawyer or go for the promotion doesn't mean you have to. Remember, this is your life and career, and nobody cares more about your career than you.

So, assuming it comes from people you trust (family, friends, colleagues, boss, mentors, coach, etc.), getting feedback can be useful because the people around you might see strengths or opportunities that you don't see in yourself. More on this later.

Finally, be willing to sit down and have a conversation with your manager (if you have one and feel comfortable) and ask about the options in front of you. Where does he or she see your career potentially going or what options might be available to you. Again, you don't have to follow your manager's advice (they may have a bias of their own), but hearing about those options can be helpful. And if you have a supportive manager, he or she might work with you to create a plan to achieve your goals.

Often, managers are not giving guidance because they don't know what you want, so the more specific you can be with your goals, the easier it will be to provide you coaching and advice. Help them help you.

Finally, once you've considered all of these options and made a decision, write it down, tell a couple of your closest friends (and your manager if you feel comfortable), and then start making a plan for how you want to get there.

If your goal is to move up the chain and earn a more senior position in the company doing something similar to what you are doing now, then your plan may be to put your head down, accept all assignments that come your way, and be the best you possibly can at your job. If you plan to switch careers entirely, you need to start writing down the steps to get you there. Who do you need to talk to? What education or skills do you need? Lots of people have dreams, but most of them never achieve them because they don't have an actual plan.

This goal and plan will come in handy when big opportunities and decisions come your way. But remember, as I said before, nothing is set in stone, and everything can change. The key is to have an idea where you are going but remain flexible so you can react when opportunities come your way.

Live Your Life for You

Remember that this is your vision, your career, and your life. So many people in this world are living their lives for other people. They have chosen jobs or careers or lifestyles to impress or appease their parents, friends, or family. They let someone else dictate what they do for work and how they live their life. That is true for every person who wanted to be an artist, musician, athlete, architect, or entrepreneur. Still, their parents told them they needed to get a "safe" or lucrative job like a doctor or lawyer or accountant.

There is nothing wrong with those jobs. Most of them pay well and provide some great security. And for some people, those jobs are their dream, and that's what they truly want to do. But many people end up in jobs because that is what their parents tell them to do, and they don't want to disappoint their parents.

I have been through this as well. And I don't want to take anything away from what your parents or family have given you or done for you. They probably raised you and fed you, and maybe they even paid for your college tuition. But unless you took out a loan from them or promised them something in return, you don't owe them anything. The entire point of this book is that you take *ownership* of your career and life and live it for you and nobody else (other than maybe a spouse and kids), so you may see me harp on this a few times.

I have been there. After college, I moved across the country and discovered entrepreneurship and tried some things that probably scared or worried my parents. I failed at many of the things I tried, and I was always worried about disappointing them. But I continued to live life for me and do what I wanted, and I have never regretted that.

I bring this up because you may be in a job or career that you don't enjoy or is not part of your long-term vision, and if this chapter has caused you to think of other things you can do, I think that's great. But you've got to be prepared for some potential judgment or pushback from your parents, family, and friends who might disagree with your decisions. Remember, this is your life, not theirs.

You can tell them that while you value their experience and advice, and you appreciate their love and support, you ultimately get to decide what you want to do with your life, and your current dream or desire is to do (insert dream here).

They may not like it, but if they love you, they will always support you.

I know this is hard, so if you need extra motivation, consider this: I strongly believe that at the end of your life, your biggest regret(s) will be the dreams you didn't fulfill and risks you didn't take. You probably won't sit around, reflecting happily on how you played it safe or did what other people (your parents) told you to do. More than likely, you'll lament the chances you didn't take, the times you didn't stand or speak up for yourself, or the times you did what other people wanted you to do instead of what you truly wanted to do.

According to the book *Top Five Regrets of the Dying* by Bronnie Ware, the number one regret people say when they reach the end is, "I wish I'd had the courage to live a life true to myself, not the life others expected of me."

That is what drives me every day and motivates me to take chances and do scary things. And this is why I continue to try to find ways to inspire and motivate others to take ownership of their careers and lives. I want you to live life for you.

What is Your Vision?

Okay, now it's your turn. What is your vision or big goal for your career? What do you really want to do? What makes you excited about the future? Where do you see yourself in ten or twenty years? Be bold but realistic (if you are thirty, you can still start a business or become a CEO, but you probably won't become a professional baseball player or astronaut).

Please take out a journal and write your ideas down before you move on. It is critical that you write something down to get the most out of this book.

Here are some examples to inspire you:

- "I want to become CFO of my company or big company"
- "Become an expert or authority in marketing"
- "Get into HR and help improve human performance in the workplace"
- "Become a stand-up comedian and make people laugh"
- "Provide value while limiting hours to spend more time traveling or with family"
- "Become more knowledgeable about business and gain experience in different functions"
- "I want to run my own business"
- "I want to retire early"

Creating New Habits

Setting a vision and goals are important, but nothing ever gets achieved without the right habits that create the action to achieve them. We will talk more about making a plan in the next chapter and establishing habits throughout the book. Be on the lookout for the habits section at the end of each chapter. That is where we can pause and reflect on the old habits that have held us back and think about the new habits that we can establish to get us where we need to go.

In this case, the old habit or way of being was to live and work in reaction mode, basing career decisions on what others tell us to do without a plan or idea of where we want to go.

The new way of being is to have a vision and purpose and idea of where we want to go (which need not be set in stone), and the new habit is to reflect on this vision and have conversations regularly to get feedback. So, here's how it looks.

Old habit: Living life in reaction mode and not ever thinking about where your career is going. Drifting with the wind and blindly doing what you're told.

New habit: Taking time on a weekly or daily basis to think about your career goals, where you want to go, how you want to get there, and whether you are making sufficient progress. You may want to go a step further and keep a journal (more on this later) to write down ideas, goals, and track progress.

Refining and Getting Feedback

Ideally, you'll have some great ideas here. Refine them down to two or three and think about what is most important for you to achieve. Only you know the answer. But as was mentioned earlier, you can also seek feedback from colleagues or friends. Ideally, you will do this exercise with one of them (if you haven't told your colleagues and friends about this book, please share it, and ask them to do the exercise with you). That will help you with feedback and accountability. Bonus!

When you have your answers or if you need help, be sure to join our free Facebook Group and share what you've come up with or where you need help.

Head over to **ownyourcareerownyourlife.com** to get the link and some other free bonuses.

CHAPTER SUMMARY AND KEY TAKEAWAYS

In this chapter, we discussed the importance and benefits of having a vision and knowing where you are going. Remember, you would not get into your car or start walking somewhere without a destination in mind. Pilots don't start flying planes without a specific destination and a plan to get there.

You may not know exactly where you want to go, but the more clarity you have, the easier it becomes to make career decisions along the way.

Set your vision by spending time writing down the things you enjoy doing, the goals you have for your career, your priorities and values, and where you might want to be or what you might want to be doing in five years. Check in with friends, colleagues, or family members that you trust and whose opinions you value to get their advice and feedback.

Remember that things will change, so don't worry about being held to what you write down. You can always change it, and nobody is going to judge or grade you.

Finally, remember that nobody cares more about your career than you do and that you need to live your life for you and nobody else. It's possible your parents may not like or agree with your career choices, but that's okay. They have their careers or lives, and you have yours, and though you can and should remain grateful for all they have done for you, the fact remains that you do not owe them anything (gasp).

Now that you have a vision and direction for your career, we will talk about the importance of connecting to a purpose before setting goals and making a plan. Let's go!

CHAPTER TWO

CONNECT TO PURPOSE

We have already talked a lot about having a vision and the benefits of getting clear on where you want to go with your career. The next step is to figure out *why*. Why do you want to achieve that big goal? Why do you want to get into marketing or finance or HR or become an entrepreneur or the CEO of your company? And why do you show up to work each day?

The answer to that last question is usually something quick and snarky like "to collect a paycheck" or "because they pay me to show up every day" or "because I have to if I want to keep my job."

But those are cop-out answers. We want to look deeper. It has been proven that the more connected we are with a purpose or our "why," the more motivated we are to work hard, engage and, go after our goals, and the more fulfilled we'll be as well.

Simon Sinek and the Golden Circles

People have been asking about the meaning of life for generations, but I think the idea of purpose and knowing your "why" in business took off and became mainstream after Simon Sinek gave his wildly popular TEDx talk called *How Great Leaders Inspire Action* (also known as The Golden Circles) in September 2009. As I write this, Sinek's talk has over forty-eight million views and counting. He subsequently published a popular book called *Start with Why* in 2009 and has since gone on to publish five successful books (including *The Infinite Game*) and speaks regularly at conferences around the world.

In Simon Sinek's TEDx talk and subsequent book, he says that people are a lot more inspired by a "why" or purpose than they are by a "what" or "how." In the talk, he says over and over that people "don't buy what you do; they buy why you do it."

This applies to the work you do and how you explain it to others. It even applies to what you tell yourself about your job or career. Hearing and understanding the "why" is much more compelling than the what or how. It can also be a strong motivator for getting things done.

When Simon Sinek gave that talk, he was speaking mostly about successful companies like Apple or pioneers like the Wright Brothers and Martin Luther King Jr. It also works to get employees to do things as well. If you think about it, you are probably a lot more motivated to do something your boss asks you to do if you understand the reason and the impact it might have on the department and organization.

Conversely, when someone (boss, colleague, friend, parent) asks (or demands) that we do something, and we have no idea why, that's when we start grumbling about doing work with no purpose. For example, your boss comes to you and asks you to spend a couple of hours running a report without an explanation, and you have no idea what the report will be used for or even see how it could be beneficial or valuable. You are probably less motivated to get it done than if you know the reason. If you know your boss will use that report to present data to his or her boss to show the value of the work you are doing in your department, it might mean something.

Connecting to Purpose Helps You Achieve Goals

We talked earlier about setting a vision, and for some, that might be to stay on the track you are on now and get a promotion. For others, it might mean big changes (like a new career) and a lot of hard work (like getting a graduate degree or learning new skills). When it comes to hard work, you may find yourself more motivated if you know your purpose or the "why" behind what you want to accomplish.

For example, when I decided to write this book, I knew it would be a big undertaking. The average nonfiction book is 50,000 words, which is a lot of writing for someone who has never written a book before. And since I already run a business and have a family and other responsibilities, I knew I would not get it done without strong motivation and setting time aside. I'll explain later how I got it done, but let's stick with the "why" for now.

If I didn't have a strong sense of "why" I was doing this, it would be easy to quit. What's the point of all this work? But

I do know why. I know I have an opportunity to get my message out and impact the lives of my friends and people like you. And I know that writing a book could also help catapult my career and business. Not to mention it will be part of my legacy and something I can show my kids and grandkids. So, I need to get this done.

Another classic example is going to the gym and getting in shape. So many people struggle with this, and everyone is on their own journey. Unless you have clear goals and a purpose or "why" behind your commitment to exercise (or do anything hard), it will be easier to give up when challenges get in the way. Your why could be wanting to live a long, healthy life or look good in the mirror or play with your kids when you're old (all of those are mine), or it could just be fitting into a dress or suit for an upcoming wedding. All of those things count and can motivate you to keep going.

Connecting Purpose to Your Job or Career

Here's where things get interesting. Besides writing books or hitting the gym, you have a job to do. And it's important to know why you show up to work every day. Remember those easy answers I mentioned earlier? Those are not the *real* answers. Because if you live in the United States or Europe or most countries in the world with a democracy (and even some without), you get to choose where you work and how you live your life. You get to choose whether you show up to work every day. Amazingly a lot of people forget about their freedom of choice.

So, let's look beneath the surface. Why do you show up to your job or business every day? Why do you want to get a promotion or move to finance or become CEO one day?

It could be because you enjoy it or want to prove to your parents and others that you can accomplish big things. There could be so many great reasons. And if you don't enjoy what you are doing, then you need to be honest about it. Most likely, you show up not because you have to (nobody is making you) or for the money, but instead, you show up every day because you are too scared to try something else or make changes.

Many people hate their jobs because what they do doesn't align with their purpose or doesn't energize them. They feel stuck because they are afraid to try anything else or even have a conversation with their manager about what they enjoy and don't enjoy about the job.

Some people are not that passionate about their jobs, but they like their boss, the money, the company, or the hours. Their real purpose is to make enough money to provide for their family and then be there for them every evening and every weekend. That's great too.

There is no judgment and no grading here. Your purpose is for you. But you need to know it. Because that purpose is why you show up to work or why you want to make that career change. It's also the thing that will motivate you to work harder and get your job done, achieve your goals, and get promoted.

Connecting to Company or a Greater Purpose

We have been talking about your purpose or "why," but there is also a great benefit in connecting with your company's purpose or a higher societal purpose. Because what you do and where you work might not be about you and your purpose. Maybe you show up because you believe strongly in what your company is doing or how they can impact the world with your help.

Recently, I spoke at an HR conference in Nashville and had lunch with a group of people before giving my talk on preparing for a future career change. I asked each of them if they were connected to a purpose or why they do what they do. One man told me he currently works as a manager, but his big goal is to become a Chief HR Officer (CHRO) one day and so he shows up with passion, purpose, and ambition to achieve that goal. Another man at our table told me he feels strongly about combating climate change. So he has chosen to work for a government entity because he feels like he can make more of a difference and an impact than he could in a private company.

It's rare, but I'm always impressed when a company helps its people find their purpose and connect it to the company's purpose. My friend, Travis Dommert, has helped orchestrate this at a large healthcare organization in Atlanta. When I interviewed him for my podcast, Travis was running workshops for all employees in the organization to discover their purpose, practice talking about it, and connect it to the company's values and purpose.

Travis said that people need a "why" behind their work to motivate them and that when an employee's purpose aligns with the values and purpose of their company, their commitment and productivity go up. When they are not aligned, that commitment and productivity go down.

Can you relate?

Most people don't have a personal purpose. But many companies have a purpose or social cause they support, and it's more than okay to hitch your purpose to theirs if you agree or it aligns with your own personal mission, purpose or values. No matter what your job is, you can always connect it to something meaningful. You are making an impact. And if you don't believe you are, then it could be time to look for another job or career.

How to Determine Your Purpose

How can we figure out our purpose or why? A lot of it goes back to your life experiences, how you were raised, and your values. What do you care about, and what energizes you?

If you are searching for your purpose, you can start by thinking back through your upbringing and past experiences and what is truly important and unique to you. Then go back to that vision or goals that you set in the previous chapter and review where you want to go. How do they connect?

Then think about your company's purpose and the role you play in that. Do you know the importance and impact of your role and the impact your company is making in the world?

Finally, realize that your purpose does not have to be grand and doesn't need to impress anyone. You don't have to be Martin Luther King Jr. or Elon Musk, trying to change the world. Your purpose is only for you. It can be to provide flawless accounting services to make your colleagues' jobs easier, to perform at the highest level so you are continuously recognized and promoted, or it can be to do your job at your highest ability to contribute to the overall success of the company and contribute to the overall strategy. There is no judgment here. The most important thing is that it is something you can refer back to often, and it gets you excited to come to work or, at the very least, answers the question, "Why am I going to work today?"

If the only answer to that question is, "Because they pay me," you are heading for boredom, burnout, or complacency. Having a purpose can help drive you when things get challenging (and they will), so I recommend you spend some time considering yours.

Now It's Your Turn

Take some of the suggestions below and brainstorm ideas for your purpose. What and who are the most important things in your life? Do you know your company's purpose? Do you or your company contribute to charities or social causes? What drives you to go to work every day? Write some of your answers down in a notebook and refine them and keep them handy for those challenging times.

It is so important not only to write this down but to tell other people and get feedback. I mentioned that I interviewed Travis about how he implemented this at his company, and he said that after his people craft their purpose, they spend a full day sharing it with others in the room, getting feedback, and then making adjustments.

That is because something that may sound okay to you in your head may not make sense to others. Or maybe they can see how your face lights up or shies away when you talk about certain things. Of course, you need to share with people you can trust. If you have good friends, they will want to help. And if you can do this with a colleague or team member, that's even better.

Once you have your purpose nailed down, write it out one more time and place it where you can refer back to it. You may also want to memorize it and recite it to yourself often so you can be sure of your purpose, where you are going, and why you do what you do.

I recite my purpose as part of my affirmations every single morning. It's a great reminder of just that—who I am, where I'm going, and why I do what I do. If you want to hear it again:

"My life's purpose is to love and support my family, continue to grow and improve, model a healthy and intentional lifestyle, help people do the best work of their lives, and add value to the world."

And my mission is to fulfill my true potential so that I can help and inspire others to do the same.

Time to rework some habits.

Old Habit: Living and working without a clear purpose or "why."

New Habit: Reflecting regularly on your purpose (or "why") and asking yourself if you feel connected to your work. Memorizing your purpose and reciting it regularly.

CHAPTER SUMMARY AND KEY TAKEAWAYS

Knowing your purpose and being able to connect it to your work and your company's values and purpose is important, yet most people don't know theirs. They go through life drifting and unsure of why they are doing things.

You can improve your determination, focus, energy, engagement, and even your peace of mind by establishing your purpose and increase your productivity by connecting it to your company's purpose or values.

Your purpose does not need to be grand (like changing the world), and it need not be judged or approved by others. Your purpose only matters to you.

Be sure to write down your purpose, share with others to get feedback, and recite it to yourself regularly.

In the next chapter, we will start to set goals and make a plan for the next steps in your career.

CHAPTER THREE

MAKE A PLAN

We've talked a lot about setting a vision and having a purpose. The vision, or big goal, tells you where you want to go (with the understanding that things will likely change), and your purpose (or "why") will help you stay motivated and remind you why you are showing up and putting in the work each day. But those two things are not enough.

It has been said that a goal without a plan is merely a wish. There is nothing wrong with wishes, but I would rather have a plan for achieving my goals rather than sitting around tossing coins into a fountain, hoping my wishes might come true.

That sounds silly, and yet that is what so many people are doing (metaphorically speaking). They have dreams or hopes or goals, but they never make a real plan or put in the hard work to achieve them. It's not enough to want a promotion, make more money, lose weight, or change careers. We have to have a plan for how we'll get there.

The plan does not have to be a long, complicated, multi-faceted strategy. But every mission has a plan. Elon Musk wants to use his company, SpaceX, to take people to Mars, and he has a very specific plan for how they are going to get there. When you get on a plane to fly to New York or Chicago (or wherever you're going), the pilots have a flight plan they follow, and they anticipate any challenges that might come up along the way. And of course, anytime you hop in your car to drive somewhere, you generally have a plan for how to get there, whether you look up the directions on Google Maps or you already know the route by memory.

So, let's revisit a real career example from earlier. Jennifer currently works in finance, but she really wants to work in HR and eventually become head of HR for a small or medium-sized organization. What should she do?

The first step might be networking with everyone who works in HR in her current organization to find out what their jobs are like and build relationships so that if and when there are job openings, they call her. She may also want to start networking with HR professionals outside her company to learn about their roles, and what types of jobs are out there. It also helps her build relationships, so it's easier to get that job later when she's ready to move.

She can also start educating herself by reading books, watching videos, taking courses, and joining membership communities that offer education and a network in that space. She could even consider going back to school to get an advanced degree in this subject.

Finally, she could have conversations with her manager about her desired career change and make a plan together for how she's going to get there. Her manager might have ideas, referrals, or recommendations. Every situation is different, but I know that nothing changes without action and conversations.

What Goes into Your Plan?

We know we need a plan, and the more detailed our plan, the more likely we are to achieve our goal. So, what goes into the plan?

Start by writing down all the ideas you can think of—things that will help you achieve that goal (networking, reading, courses, company resources, etc.) and the people who can help you. Then map them out and break the goals down into smaller quarterly, monthly, or weekly goals.

If your big goal is to move to HR, and one of the habits you want to establish to get you there is to network with HR professionals to learn about their jobs, you could set a goal to have lunch or coffee with at least two people per month.

Then, and most importantly, write down the first thing you can do to get started. Often, when people set big goals, they get overwhelmed with everything they need to do and then start procrastinating.

One of the biggest and best methods for beating procrastination is to start taking action right away. If your goal is to run a marathon, you need a plan for how to train and work up to 26.2 miles. But once you have that plan, the next best thing to do is to start running. You'll never make progress on that goal until you lace up your shoes and take that first step.

Create SMART Goals

One of the most important things you can do is take that big vision, dream, or goal and break it down into smaller goals. These goals should be as specific as possible and set up in a SMART way.

There have been thousands of books, articles, and other things written about SMART goals, and chances are, you already know what they are. If not, I'll give a brief overview.

SMART goals are goals that are Specific, Measurable, Achievable (some say Actionable), Realistic, and Time-bound or Timely.

Why set SMART goals? Because when goals are non-specific and cannot be measured, they often don't get done. A goal like "I want to lose weight" or "I want to change careers" is not very specific, difficult to take action on, and measure. How much weight? Also, without a schedule or deadline, procrastination will often set in. That's why having a timeline is so important. How much weight do you want to lose by when?

In this example, many people say, "I want to lose weight," but they never do because they don't know where or how to start. Or, they give up because there is no specificity or accountability. Instead, it would be better to say, "I want to lose twenty pounds in the next three months by cutting out sugar from my diet and exercising four or five times per week."

That is a goal that is specific, measurable, achievable, realistic, and timely. It doesn't mean it's not difficult, but with some help and accountability, you can do it.

SMART GOALS

SMART

SPECIFIC	MEASURABLE	ACHIEVABLE	REALISTIC	TIMELY
WHAT DO YOU WANT TO DO?	HOW WILL YOU KNOW WHEN YOU'VE REACHED IT?	IS IT IN YOUR POWER TO ACCOMPLISH IT?	CAN YOU REALISTICALLY ACHIEVE IT?	WHEN EXACTLY DO YOU WANT TO ACCOMPLISH IT?

Let's go back to the career change example. One of the big things we talked about was networking with HR professionals. So, the SMART goal could be, "I want to have conversations with four HR professionals a month for the next six months." That is specific, measurable, very achievable, realistic, and timely. You could also say, "My goal is to read two HR-related books a month for the next six months." That meets the requirements as well.

Another example is someone who says, "I want to make more money," but they never do because they don't know where or how to start, or give up because there is no specificity or accountability. Instead, it would be better to say, "I make more money by achieving a promotion to senior manager by March 15 by meeting with my manager regularly and taking weekly action on all the requirements to earn that promotion."

Examples:

Let's look at a few more examples to help you get started:

- I want to complete a certification course by March 1, and I will do that by attending classes or watching videos three times a week

- I want to get my CPA by September 1 by completing a course, doing homework and passing the exam

- I want to take at least one extra project at work each month, which will give me more experience and exposure

- I will study finance for an hour, three nights a week, for the next four months to increase my knowledge and achieve a certification

- My goal is to get promoted in six months, and I will have regular conversations with my manager throughout that time to make sure I'm on track

- My goal is to get a job in HR by December 1, and I will get there networking with at least three HR professionals each month and having regular conversations with my manager

- I will find a mentor by speaking with at least ten people who have the job I want and asking at least three of them if they will mentor me

- I will learn more about what's going on in my field and build my network by joining an association and attending at least four conferences a year

There are many great resources out there to help you set and achieve your goals. One of my favorites is the book *Your Best Year Ever* by Michael Hyatt. He also has an online course by the same name, and I have used both to set and achieve big goals over the years.

Another book I love on this subject is *The Miracle Equation* by Hal Elrod. I read that book twice and used the teachings and formula to create and sell out my first conference, the Talent Development Think Tank, which I hosted with my friend Bennett Phillips.

What's Your Plan?

Now it's time to craft your plan. Take out a journal and write down everything you think could help you achieve that vision or goal you wrote down earlier. Then turn some of them into SMART goals. Remember to make them Specific, Measurable, Achievable, Realistic, and Time-bound. Finally, write down one or two things you can do right away to get you started, and then take action.

Once you've written down all your goals and steps, it would be helpful for you to again share this plan with a friend, colleague, and especially your manager (if you're comfortable).

When you share your goals and plans with people you trust and respect, you can get feedback that might help you refine those plans and set you in the right direction.

By the way, you can do this with any journal, but I created the *Own Your Career Own Your Life Companion Journal* as a companion to this book and to help you achieve your goals. If you don't want to get that one, two others I have used and love are *The Freedom Journal* by John Lee Dumas and *The Full Focus Planner* by Michael Hyatt.

CHAPTER SUMMARY AND KEY TAKEAWAYS

Remember that a goal without a plan is just a wish. Just like when you get in your car or board a plane, you need a plan for achieving your vision or goals. It should include some SMART goals and milestones. What can you do on a weekly or monthly basis to help you make progress toward your big goal?

Once you've written down some goals, share them with friends, colleagues, and your manager to get feedback. Then refine them and start taking action. That first step is the most important because it will allow you to start making progress right away.

CHAPTER FOUR

ASKING FOR AND GETTING HELP

There is an old African proverb that says, "If you want to go fast, go alone, but if you want to go far, go together." And it's true. If you want to achieve significant success and go far in your career, you will need help.

Asking for and getting help is critically important and often dismissed or overlooked. It may seem obvious to most people, but humans are social creatures, and we are not meant to go through life alone. Similarly, there are very few self-made leaders who have achieved success all on their own. Most people (including me) have had a ton of help along the way.

Yet, many people have a hard time asking for help. Why? I think the biggest reason is that we believe it might make us look weak or like we can't figure things out on our own, so we are somehow less successful. But of course, those things are entirely untrue.

There is nobody on Earth who has it all figured out or knows everything. We all need help. And most people enjoy helping others. I do, and I'm guessing you do as well. It makes us feel significant, altruistic, and let's be honest; it's an ego boost. So why do we avoid asking for help when we know we need it?

I think it comes down to fear and ego. We often avoid asking for help because we are either embarrassed to share our goals or feel ashamed to admit that we can't figure things out on our own. But it's silly because not only do we all need help, but we all love helping others. I have been guilty of trying to do things on my own (it's something I am still working on), yet I have achieved so much in my career and life because of the help I've received.

I remember when I was in business school at USC, I wasn't sure what career I wanted to get into after I graduated. So, I started reaching out to alumni who had jobs I was interested in (finance, strategy, operations, marketing) and asked them if they'd get on the phone or have coffee with me and tell me about their careers. I reached out to about thirty alumni expecting maybe half to agree. But I was shocked when nearly all of them got back to me and agreed to talk. In fact, I don't think I received one rejection. Why? Because people love to help others, especially if there is some association (same school, a friend of a friend, etc.).

At the end of nearly all of those "information interviews," the person I spoke with would ask me how they can help further and if I wanted them to make more intros. It was amazing. It still happens to me all the time. I connect with new people constantly, especially people in my field of Talent Development, and at the end of almost every new conversation, the person I'm speaking with asks how they can help me. So, I often ask for introductions, and they almost always oblige. That is one way I've grown such a big network and learned so much about talent development.

You Never Know Where It Will Lead

The other amazing thing about asking people for help is that you never know where it might lead. In 2010, I worked as a product manager for a large insurance company, and I was not very happy about my job or career. The job didn't leverage my strengths and was not very engaging or interesting for me. I was drifting, unfulfilled, and had no vision or purpose connected to what I did. I also wasn't making as much money as I thought I could or should.

I thought that getting into sales might be a good idea since I loved talking to people, and I had heard and read that sales careers provided more autonomy (something I wanted) and the opportunity to make a lot more money. Plus, I figured that having sales experience would always be helpful for my career. But I honestly had no idea where to start or what to do.

So, I sent an email to my friend Adam, who I knew had spent most of his career in sales. Adam was a friend I met through business school. We did not know each other well, but we had had a few conversations, and I knew he had a lot of sales experience. I sent him an email to ask for his advice.

It turned out that Adam had just started working for a cool consulting company called BTS in San Francisco six months earlier and thought I might be a good fit for a consulting role there. That email led to several conversations, a referral, and eventually, an interview and a job offer from BTS. A few months later, I accepted an offer and moved with my wife to San Francisco to start a new career in a dream job with BTS as a consultant.

That one email and request for help led to a new job and career that I loved and an opportunity to travel around the world and develop a ton of new amazing friendships, which led me to where I am today.

If I had not asked Adam for help, I would never have found that job, and I have no idea what I'd be doing today, but I would likely not be in consulting or writing this book!

Life is a journey full of twists and turns, and you never know where things will go, but you also will miss out on tons of opportunities if you aren't willing to ask for help.

As my career progressed, I built my business and personal brand, and I launched podcasts because I had help from friends. Notably, when I launched my first podcast *(The Entrepreneur Hot Seat)* in 2017, I got a ton of help from friends who already had podcasts.

I'm only able to write, publish, and market this book because of all the advice and help I've received from friends. Most notably, I invested in a course from my friend, Honorée Corder (author of several books including *You Must Write a Book*), to learn everything I need to know about writing, publishing, and marketing a book successfully. She has published over fifty books, so why would I try to figure everything out myself when I can hire her and ask her for help?

I'm also in mastermind groups, hire coaches, and ask other friends for help all the time. I have been historically great at building a network but not so great at sales, so I joined a mastermind group run by the fabulous Jessica Lorimer in the UK and have been working with her for more than a year. I've gotten tons of help from her as I've built my business and brand.

My wife, Cortney, and I help each other all the time in business and personal matters (of course). We are best friends, and though, like in any partnership, we've had our challenging moments (she's editing this book after all). We support each other with everything, and I wouldn't be here without her. The point is that we help each other often.

Whom to Ask

I've already talked a lot about the importance of asking for help and why it can be beneficial. You never know what expertise, wisdom, or tools someone might have to help you on your journey. Here are a few examples of people you could be asking for help:

- Your manager, supervisor, department head, VP, HR Business Partner (HRBP), or HR representative
- Colleague, friend, mentor, peer, direct report
- Friends, family, teachers, neighbors, etc.
- Conferences, communities, church groups, peer groups, career groups
- Coaches, counselors, professors
- Creators of podcasts, videos, books, courses, etc.

There are so many people and places that can help you on your journey. The biggest key is to get over your ego and stop thinking you should be able to figure everything out. I have several mentors and coaches and ask for help constantly. It's one of the biggest reasons for my success.

Career Conversations with Your Manager

Speaking of asking for help, if you work for a company, there is probably nobody who can help you more than your manager or supervisor. Every situation is different, and I won't get into addressing how to handle good and bad bosses (there are many of both), but you are probably going to need help from your manager to succeed.

Chances are, your manager wants you to succeed (because that will help him or her succeed). But frequently, managers don't know how to coach or mentor their direct reports because they don't know what their employees want.

Going back to our earlier conversations, the more specific you can get with your goals, the easier it is to ask for and receive help.

If your manager knows that you want a promotion, you want to move to HR, start a side project, move to a different office, or pursue some other goal; they can help you put together a plan.

It's an unfortunate fact of life, but people make a lot of assumptions in this world, and if you don't communicate what you want, they assume you are fine where you are. And I've heard that many employees are frustrated by managers' lack of guidance, but managers can't guide you if they don't know what you want to improve or where you want to go with your career. So, you've got to be prepared to take everything we worked on earlier and have a regular conversation with your manager about your vision, purpose, goals, and plan to achieve them.

In her book, *Get There Faster*, my good friend Christine DiDonato says that most managers have very little experience giving feedback or career coaching, and without guidance from the employee, they don't know how to help. Many people are waiting for these discussions and guidance from their managers, but it never comes.

Christine suggests that you need to take the initiative to start and have this conversation and explain your specific goals (that we worked on earlier). So, write down your goals and plan, and bring them to your manager for help. Unless or until your manager knows what you want, they can't help you.

If you want more guidance in this area, I recommend you check out Christine's book. As the former head of talent development at Sony Electronics and a career expert, she has coached thousands of people on these topics, so I trust her advice.

Don't Go Too Far

While you must be willing and able to ask for help along your journey, there are two things to remember. First, it's very important that you spend time helping others. Think of it as karma or a bank account. To have a healthy account, you want to deposit more than you withdraw; therefore, you should be seeking to help others as much as or more than you ask for help.

Second, try not to be needy. That means it is great to ask for help, but if you ask too much or beg people or ask for unreasonable things, it will make you look bad. There is an art to this.

If you are networking with HR leaders from other companies, it is reasonable to ask for their advice and maybe for introductions to other people. Still, it is probably not appropriate to blatantly ask them for a job.

I think about it this way, if my request is something they can do in less than ten minutes and it won't put their reputation at risk, I make the ask. Suppose it is a major effort or might put them in a difficult situation (like recommending you to their boss without knowing you well). In that case, I don't usually make the ask until I've developed a great relationship or am confident they'd be willing to do it.

Similarly, if someone provides a couple of introductions to you and those work well, you may be tempted to go back to them and ask for more. A second time may be fine, but when you come back a third time asking for even more introductions, they may start to perceive you as needy and are asking for too much of their time.

If you are reciprocating (and you always should when possible) and offering that person introductions or something else helpful, you may have enough goodwill and trust to ask for more.

A very recent example is when my friend, Rachel Richards (author of the books *Money Honey* and *Passive Income, Aggressive Retirement*), offered me some introductions to podcasts she has been on. In return, she asked me for a few introductions for podcast interviews. We have a great reciprocal arrangement.

Who Can Help You?

Now it's time to take that journal out again and write down all the people who might help you achieve your goals. It might include your manager, colleagues, peers, friends, recruiters, career coaches, family, friends of friends, professors, etc.

You can also get help from resources and people you don't even know via books, articles, blogs, podcasts, videos, courses, communities, and conferences. More on those later.

Remember, just like with your plan, it's vital to get started right away. So, pick the easiest person to talk to on your list and call, text, or email them right away to get started.

Finally, remember to be kind, generous, humble, and polite with your approach.

CHAPTER SUMMARY AND KEY TAKEAWAYS

Remember the African proverb, "If you want to go fast and do things quickly, you can certainly try them on your own, but if you want to truly go far and be successful, you need help." Start thinking of all the people who could potentially help you and then start asking. You might be surprised at the response. They are not going to judge you or think you are weak for asking for help. They might appreciate it because most people love helping others. Make that list and start asking. Just remember not to go too far or get too greedy or needy.

Your Turn

Okay, now it's your turn. Take out your journal and write down all the people you could ask for help from and tools you could leverage to learn from (podcasts, books, etc.). Who can help you on your journey, and what would be reasonable to ask of them?

Old Habit: Trying to do everything yourself and thinking you are weak if you need help.

New Habit: Seeking out and asking for help when you need it and being as helpful as possible to others.

CHAPTER FIVE

TAKING RESPONSIBILITY

There are a lot of things that happen in life and business that are completely out of our control. These might include our boss leaving, strategy and staff changes, macroeconomic forces, stock market changes, company layoffs, or a global pandemic. Change is inevitable, and we might set big goals and make the best plans, but many things can happen that are outside of our control. COVID-19 is an example of something that affected everyone, and nobody expected it. It definitely changed things for me.

In early 2020 my business was growing, and I was flying all over the United States running in-person workshops for clients with many more on the calendar. Then, when COVID-19 hit and locked everything down, my business took a hit, which forced me to stop flying and find ways to pivot.

I find that many people in these situations often want to play the victim and wait for things to improve or someone to show or tell them what to do. I spoke with several people who told me they were going to wait until things returned to "normal." But I'm a fan of taking full responsibility for everything in life, even when situations seem out of our control. That means looking at a situation, figuring out what is within our control, and then taking action.

So, in my example, I looked for opportunities to turn my in-person training into virtual training and then started reaching out and building relationships (virtually) with a lot of clients and prospects. I looked for ways to serve them. Eventually, that turned into a virtual membership community I launched in June 2020.

We've gone through a series of chapters and exercises to help you set a direction for your career and achieve your goals. But I don't think you will succeed until you take full ownership of your career and life. That means focusing on what's in your control and running your career and life as if you are an entrepreneur running a business. It also means taking responsibility for everything that happens and not waiting for others to tell you what to do.

It may be true that many people move up the ladder, get promoted, and make a lot of money without truly taking the time to plan out their career and act with intention. But I find this is not only rare but also unfulfilling. The constant uncertainty can cause stress and unhappiness.

I had found with my own life that when I started taking full ownership and responsibility for everything going on and living life on my terms, I became a lot happier and more ful-filled. Why? Because waiting for others to tell me what to do is risky and unfulfilling. And complaining and blaming others doesn't get me anywhere. It's stressful and unproductive and makes me look and feel bad.

I once heard that excuses and blaming are like a rocking chair. They give you something to do, but they don't take you anywhere. So, what did that look like for me?

As I dove deeper into this idea of taking ownership and being more intentional with my career, I started reading, learning more, and doing self-assessments to understand my strengths, weaknesses, core values, personality type, and the work I enjoy.

That's what eventually led me to the world of entrepre-neurship, wanting to be my own boss and run my own busi-ness. I value freedom more than security. I enjoy the thrill of not knowing where my next paycheck will come from (crazy, right?). I enjoy taking on new projects like writing a book—that may or may not pay off for my career.

That may not be for you, and that's great. We are all very different people. As you get to know yourself better (strengths, weaknesses, values, energizers, desires, dreams, etc.), you can update the plan for your career and then take responsibility by being intentional with your actions and time.

Let's Flip the Switch

As we discussed earlier, owning your career means taking full responsibility for your career and life with the understanding that nobody cares more about your career and life than you do. It means you stop waiting for others to tell you what to do and take action on your own dreams and goals. It means you treat your career and life like a business and you don't waste time blaming others or making excuses for why you didn't achieve things.

If you make a mistake or don't get something done, you take responsibility and figure out how to do it better next time. If an accident happens that changes your course or impedes your way, you ask what you can learn from it, how you can improve next time, or how it benefits you.

Let's look at some career examples:

Let's say you are flying somewhere for an important business meeting and the flight gets canceled because of weather or mechanical problems. The drifter gets angry and yells at the airline workers and blames others for this challenge. The responsible person immediately jumps into action and starts figuring out how to make the best of it. Can they get another flight? Can they run the meeting virtually? Can someone else from their team run the meeting? Do they need to send an email or make a phone call to the others in the meeting to let them know? Can they mitigate this risk in the future by catching an earlier flight?

Here's another example—one that happened a lot during the COVID-19 pandemic. Let's say your boss comes to you and says that the company is making some changes and your department and your job are being eliminated. You have thirty days to find another job internally, or you're going to be let go. The drifter gets angry, sad, or scared and blames the company, the executives, the boss, or the Universe and claims that this is unfair. They've done a good job, and this is how they get rewarded? The responsible person accepts the things outside of their control and takes action on the things within their control. They've been building their network and saving money just in case something like this happens.

They immediately start sending emails and making phone calls to book coffee meetings with people in other departments and friends in other companies to find out about other job opportunities. They also spend some time mapping out their options from here. Maybe this is a good opportunity to change careers or try working on their own (as an entrepreneur or consultant) or a chance to take some time off and spend more time with family.

This is not meant to mitigate emotions. It's normal to have an emotional reaction or be disappointed if you get laid off. But, the responsible person doesn't waste time blaming others. Instead, they focus on what they can control and start taking action.

Everything Happens for You

The second example above reminds me of another important principle of taking ownership and responsibility for your career and life. That is the core belief that everything happens for you, not to you. If you are not familiar with this concept or have never bought into it, let me explain in more detail.

A lot of people in our society live in reaction mode and like to play the victim when things don't go their way. If they get fired from their job, cut off in traffic, passed over for a promotion, not invited to a party, sick, injured, flight delays, too drunk at the holiday party, the stock market goes down, car accident, etc., they feel like a victim and complain that life isn't fair and that bad things always happen to them. The list of things that can happen to us in life goes on and on. All of these are opportunities to either be a victim and blame others (or the Universe) or to take responsibility and leverage the very powerful belief that everything happens for us, not to us.

What does that mean? It means that you believe deep down that everything that happens is an opportunity or even a gift. You believe there is some reason or silver lining, even if you can't see it right away. Even if there is no silver lining, you refuse to get angry or blame anyone because you know you are the one in charge of your life, and there is no point in complaining. Anger, sadness, and complaining are all forms of fighting reality. And guess who wins that fight every time?

The cool and interesting thing is that many challenges in life can often turn out to be blessings in disguise and can help set us on the right path for new opportunities.

How My Failure Turned into My Success

I mentioned earlier that my friend got me an interview that led to a job with a cool global consulting firm called BTS. I was excited about the job, and I loved many facets of it, from traveling around the world, facilitating workshops to working on different projects. Every day was different. I loved many aspects of the job, but I struggled with the detailed work of developing client solutions and was not a good project manager. Turns out, I'm not very detail-oriented.

The company had a pretty ambitious "up or out" culture for consultants who needed to be good at development, delivery (facilitation), and sales to move up and be successful. Unfortunately, I was not cutting it with the development part of the job, which led to a couple of very difficult conversations with both my manager and the head of the office at the time. The most difficult was when they sat down with me to tell me that I would not be promoted after two years as a consultant because I did not meet the development requirements.

I was extremely disappointed and definitely shed some tears in that meeting.

I had always been a very ambitious person and dreamed of moving up, getting promotions, getting recognized, making more money, and making partner one day. Possibly even running the company. But all that came crumbling down. I felt like a failure.

But as I mentioned before, everything happens *for* us, and there is almost always a silver lining. In this case, it came in the form of a new opportunity. Shortly after that difficult conversation, the head of the office, Jessica Parisi, took me to breakfast and offered me a new role in the company that was more focused on sales. It would leverage my strengths and free me up to do more of what I enjoyed and excelled at, like facilitation and sales, and less of the stuff I struggled with like project management. I am lucky she saw my "native genius" (what I'm truly good at) and was willing to create a new job for me.

I accepted the offer and embarked on a new job and trajectory that taught me many lessons about myself and my abilities. That job eventually led to me leaving BTS to join a smaller sister company as an independent consultant running my own business selling and running training and development programs for companies. That role was a great bridge and stepping-stone toward following my dream to become an entrepreneur (which I am today).

That experience also taught me a lot about my strengths: networking, building relationships, facilitating workshops, teaching, and coaching. It also taught me about my weaknesses, which include project management and any detailed work. After all the lessons, I was able to pivot and find something that allows me to live my values and spend my time leveraging my strengths and less time trying to fix my weaknesses.

Missing out on that promotion at BTS was a major disappointment, but as you can see, it was indeed a blessing in disguise, and I am grateful to Jessica. I often refer to her as the greatest "multiplier" and leader I've ever worked for, for setting me on the course I'm on now.

Over the years, I've watched many colleagues lose jobs because they did not meet the demanding requirements or were just not a good fit. It was sad and disappointing, but in almost every instance, those friends moved on to better things. The challenge of getting fired turned into an opportunity to find a job or start a business that better leveraged their strengths and allowed them to do something they enjoyed.

With the right mindset and perspective, almost any challenge can turn into an opportunity.

Now Is the Time to Take Ownership

I've been talking for several chapters now about the idea of owning your career. It ultimately comes down to taking full responsibility for it and not waiting for others to tell you what to do or blaming others when things don't go the way you want.

Now is the time to flip the switch, shift your mindset, and take full responsibility. That means focusing on things that are within your control and worrying less about the things that are not. That means doing all the things we discussed like

- writing down your vision, purpose, and goals
- making a plan
- taking the initiative for the next steps, and
- not waiting for anyone else to tell you what to do.

That also means learning from mistakes and resisting the urge to complain or blame others. In fact, I have a challenge for you. But first, I want you to take out your journal and take a few moments to write down some of the ways you can take more responsibility in your career. Maybe you can start volunteering for more projects or initiating conversations with your manager or peers. Maybe you can start taking online classes or applying for that job you've wanted. Or maybe, it just means avoiding a victim mindset and eliminating complaining from your life. Here's that challenge.

The No Complaining Challenge

Complaining is pretty common for most people, especially in the corporate world. But if you think about it, complaining rarely helps anyone. I mean, if you complain about your food to the server at a restaurant, you might get a free meal, but other than that, I've never seen complaining do much for anyone except make them miserable.

So, my challenge to you is to eliminate complaining for thirty days and see how you feel. If you are a habitual complainer, this may take practice, and you may have to take it one day at a time. But try to catch yourself whenever you are complaining about something, and take notice when others around you do it.

Do it and see how you feel. If you feel better about your life and career (and I think you will), I invite you to keep it up. If you don't notice any changes, you miss complaining, and you decide I'm full of crap, then, by all means, go back to complaining (and you can even complain about this challenge and book if you want – it's your life).

This one change has added so much value to my life and made me a much happier person. I still catch myself complaining sometimes but for the most part I have stopped and I find I am much happier as a result.

Tip: Complainers love hanging around other complainers, so this may be extra difficult if all your friends are complainers. You may find that when you stop, they don't like you as much. If you want to attract more positive, ambitious, successful people in your life, you'll want to stop complaining and start taking more responsibility.

So, take the thirty-day no complaining challenge and be sure to let me know how it goes.

CHAPTER SUMMARY

Many people in life are drifting. They are waiting for others to tell them what to do—their parents, boss, and even friends. They avoid responsibility and spend most of their time reacting and complaining about others. But that is no longer going to be you because you are going to start taking full responsibility for your life and career (if you haven't already).

That means owning your career, learning from your mistakes (and the mistakes of others), writing down a plan, being intentional with your actions, and aligning those actions with your values and purpose.

This is going to be exciting. But taking full responsibility does not mean you can do everything on your own. To be successful, you'll need some help.

CHAPTER SIX

THE TIME IS NOW TO OWN YOUR CAREER

Now that we've covered some of the steps to owning your career, I want to finish this section by imploring you to shift your thinking and start taking action. Regardless of how old or experienced you are, there is no better time to take ownership of your career and your life!

Many people out there are drifting along, waiting for their boss to give them their next assignment, or complaining about not getting that promotion they want without having a real conversation with their manager to find out exactly what they need to do. Too many assumptions are being made. Don't let this be you!

You may be thinking about your career so far and lamenting over some mistakes you've made. That's normal, but don't let it slow you down. We all make mistakes. I've made plenty. You need to realize they are all part of the journey to get you to where you are in your career, and where you are now is perfect.

You can't change the past, but you can take control of the present and start taking action to build your future.

In the next section of this book, I will show you the things you can start doing now to own your future and prepare for whatever comes (job changes, layoffs, future work, new opportunities, etc.).

You have to start by shifting your mindset and understanding that you own your career. Nobody else is responsible, and nobody else cares as much as you do. Not your mom, not your sister, not your boss, or even your significant other. Nobody.

That means you have to decide what your vision and goals are, what your purpose is, and then make a plan for how you will utilize the limited time you have to achieve those things.

What actions can you start taking to set you up for a career of happiness, fulfillment, and success? Take out your journal and write some of them down now.

Old Habit: Drifting along, waiting for others to tell you what to do with your career and daily job.

New Habit: Starting each day and week with intention and being proactive with everything you do with the knowledge of how it's moving you toward your goals.

In the next section, we will start preparing for the future, and whatever may come. Let's go!

PART II

Take Control of Your Future

The first part of this book was all about taking ownership of your career. We started with setting a vision for where you want to go and then spent time connecting that vision and your work with your values and purpose. Then, we talked about making a plan and setting goals to help you achieve your big dreams. Most importantly, we talked about taking responsibility for your career and not waiting for others to tell you what to do or where to work.

When I first started talking about setting a vision and making a plan, I used the analogy of the pilot flying the plane or even you driving to the grocery store. You have to know your destination before you can start flying or driving. It's critical.

But just because you have a destination in mind and spent time setting goals and making plans for how to get there, doesn't mean things will always work out perfectly. If you've been alive for a while, you've probably noticed that life has a way of throwing wrenches in your plans. And when you are planning things more than a few months away, things almost always change.

You might set a course to drive to the grocery store or visit a friend and anticipate it will take twenty minutes, but maybe there is an accident or road closure, and you have to take a detour. Or maybe, the grocery store is closed, or your friend isn't home, and you have to change plans.

When I started writing this book in January 2020, we were in a booming economy, and my business was taking off. As I review the first draft in April, we are in the middle of a global pandemic with travel grounded and businesses closed. Things change, and we often can't predict what's coming.

The famous (and sometimes controversial) boxing champion, Mike Tyson, famously said, "Everyone has a plan until they get punched in the mouth."

I love this quote and metaphor because it vividly reminds us that we can all make plans, but things will happen along the way to knock us off our path. So, it's critical to prepare for whatever might come.

The unanticipated changes might include things like a company strategy changing, your job being eliminated or changed, getting fired, getting promoted, your manager leaving, new job opportunities popping up, a spouse wanting to move, a new baby or other personal life change that causes you to reflect and want to make changes in your plan.

In life and business (and especially in our careers), we cannot predict the future. So, I think it's very important to do what will set you up for success if and when things change.

That includes things like continuous learning, building a network, and building a personal and professional brand. We'll walk through each of these in this section and discuss how you can use them to prepare for future career changes and all the things that can come up.

Whether you are twenty-two and just starting your career or fifty-five and in the prime of your career, you owe it to yourself to prepare for the future because quite honestly, we never really know what the future will bring and what your job will look like five or ten years from now.

Are you ready?

CHAPTER SEVEN

THE FUTURE OF WORK

Before we get into how to prepare for the "future of work," I want to tell you why you should be thinking about it.

You may not have stopped to take a look around and think about it, but the world of work is changing fast. The rate of change has never been faster than it is now. And yet, it will also never be slower than it is today. That means the rate of change will only get faster, and therefore, more difficult to keep up with if you're not prepared.

That was a statement I wrote and spoke about before COVID-19 completely changed the world and how we work.

Before COVID, I was flying around the US for in-person meetings and workshops, but now everything I do is virtual, with several meetings per day on Zoom. I also host two podcasts, use social media every day, and can run my entire business from anywhere on my iPhone. These are all things that I could not even dream of twenty years ago.

When I got my first cell phone in 2001, I only used it for two things: make phone calls and play that snake game when I was bored (I miss that game). Today, I use my phone to take and edit photos, post on social media, keep up with friends, answer emails, play podcasts and music, check in for flights, buy stocks, order a ride, buy virtually anything (thanks Amazon), and settle almost every argument (with Wikipedia's help, of course).

This is not a book about technology or how the world economy is changing. But, think about how much it has changed the way we work. Using this technology, most of us can now work from anywhere, anytime. And the technology has created new businesses and jobs you couldn't imagine twenty years ago, like podcasting. And this has all been accelerated by COVID-19 and the need for almost everyone to work remotely.

In fact, before COVID there were many companies that refused to let their employees work remotely and insisted that people must be in the office to be productive. Once COVID hit, everyone went remote and productivity actually went up, not down, and the world of work was forever changed.

New technology and the way we work has also eliminated many jobs and professions. There are many toll roads where I live, and when I was growing up, my dad had to stop at each toll booth and either drop exact change in the basket or hand a bill to a toll operator and get change. Now, I have a transponder in my car that automatically charges me as I drive through the toll "collector" at seventy miles per hour. Before COVID, there were a few toll collectors left, but I'm guessing those jobs will never come back.

Those are just a few in a million examples I could give of jobs being eliminated by technology. But technology also creates new jobs and businesses. For example, I recently hired my friend Lauren Davis to manage social media for my conference, the Talent Development Think Tank. Almost every company now has a Social Media Manager or an entire team managing social media. Those jobs didn't even exist ten plus years ago.

So, we can see that jobs are changing as fast as the economy and many jobs that exist today probably won't exist ten years from now. There will also be a whole list of jobs and businesses that exist ten years from now that we could've never even imagined today.

Many people (including me) believe we are heading toward more of a "gig" economy where more people are doing project-based work either as outside consultants or inside companies. I don't think we truly know where things will go, but I know the COVID-19 pandemic accelerated the move toward remote and virtual work, and things continue to change all the time. I think it's pretty certain that the traditional career as we know it has forever changed.

There are many books out there about the "future of work" and the "fourth Industrial Revolution," so I won't go too deep into predictions or what the future of work will look like. Suffice it to say that things are changing fast and are going to keep changing. And we want to be ready.

That's why we have to do everything we can to stay relevant and prepare for the future. We want to be ready when things change. So, let's talk about how to do that.

CHAPTER EIGHT

INVEST IN CONTINUOUS LEARNING

If you are not growing, you might be doing the opposite. I firmly believe that humans have a need and capacity to keep learning throughout our lives. And as I already said, the business world is always changing, so if we are not investing time in learning new things (trends, methods, rules, best practices, etc.), we might fall behind or be disrupted.

Many people think they are done learning once they finish school, but I think that is just the beginning, and the most successful people are the ones who continue to invest in learning throughout their careers.

Be Like a Doctor or Accountant

In the talks that I give on preparing for your next career change, I often advise people to be more like a doctor or accountant. Why? Because unlike many other professions, doctors and accountants have continuous learning requirements. They must spend a certain number of hours learning each year to keep up with the latest rules, regulations, trends, and best practices.

There are quite a few professions—doctor, nurse, lawyer, architect, accountant, tax preparer, social workers—that require continuous learning. The same day I was writing this section, my neighbor and architect, Mark, stopped by and mentioned he was spending his week doing his "continuous learning," required to keep his license.

But unlike his job as an architect, most jobs and professions do not require continuous learning. Some professions, like HR, have certifications that require continuous learning, but those certifications are optional and more like badges of honor than requirements to do the job.

For most people, learning and improvement are provided by an employer or not done at all. The majority of us wait for someone else to tell us what to do or learn or even refuse these opportunities when they are offered. There are no requirements, so they go through their careers hoping their knowledge and job stays relevant. But we already know from our conversation about how work is changing, that those who don't choose to invest in learning are doomed to fall behind and potentially become obsolete.

Luckily, you are not most people. You are not only doing the minimum required or waiting for your boss to tell you what to do; you are ready to take the initiative and keep learning to prepare for the future of work.

Prioritizing Learning

Life is busier than ever, and there is an endless list of things to do. Emails never stop coming, new projects are starting weekly, and social media never stops. Oh, and you have a life too. Unless you prioritize and make time for learning, it probably won't happen (sound familiar?).

There are some great companies out there that encourage their employees to take time out from work to learn or improve, but I have found those companies are few and far between. That's why it is up to you to take responsibility for your learning and growth. It is up to you to find the best knowledge and methods for learning so you can continue to learn, grow, improve, and be qualified for the jobs of the future (or the new job you want).

How do you keep learning when you have so many other things to do? You have to make it a priority. That means it is more important than other things, and you schedule time to get it done. Because if you don't prioritize it or schedule time, it likely won't get done, and you will fall behind. And trust me, I know there will always be more urgent things to do than sit down, read a book, listen to a podcast, or take a class. But just because those other things seem urgent does not make them more important.

That's why you need to make learning a priority and schedule time weekly for some learning or development activity.

Eisenhower Matrix

If you've ever heard of the Eisenhower Matrix, you know that the work and learning we are talking about fall into the Important-Not-Urgent quadrant (see example below). President Dwight D. Eisenhower invented this matrix (and it was later popularized by Stephen Covey in his book *Seven Habits of Highly Effective People*) to help him (and others) plan and prioritize which actions to focus on.

Most people spend the bulk of their time in the urgent quadrants, which means they are almost always reacting to requests and putting out metaphorical fires. But as Eisenhower and Covey would tell you, those are not the best places to be. The best places to spend your time are in the "important" quadrants and specifically the Important, Not-Urgent quadrant, where you can give ample time to important things without being rushed.

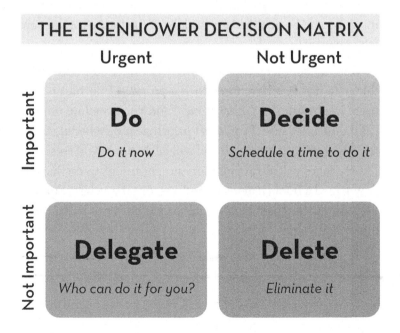

THE EISENHOWER DECISION MATRIX

	Urgent	Not Urgent
Important	**Do** *Do it now*	**Decide** *Schedule a time to do it*
Not Important	**Delegate** *Who can do it for you?*	**Delete** *Eliminate it*

I would put continuous learning in this Important, Not-Urgent quadrant. But first, you have to understand the importance and purpose, or you'll never do it. Something else will always come up.

Sharpening the Saw

We know the world of work is constantly changing and it's important to invest in continuous learning. But I know there will always be more urgent things that pop up, so I want to tell you a story about a couple of lumberjacks.

Two lumberjacks decided to have a competition to see who could cut down more trees and saw up more wood in a day. The first lumberjack started cutting and never stopped for the rest of the day. The second lumberjack stopped every hour for fifteen minutes. The first lumberjack kept hearing his competitor stopping and became very confident he would win. But at the end of the day, the second lumberjack had cut way more wood.

"How can that be? I heard you stop several times while I continued to cut the entire day!" exclaimed the first lumberjack.

"I was stopping to rest and sharpen my saw and was able to cut more wood as a result," replied the second.

Stephen Covey also popularized a similar story in his book *The 7 Habits of Highly Effective People*. In that book, the seventh habit is called "Sharpen the Saw" because, as Covey explains, it is important for us to stop and rest, renew, learn, and connect with others. Doing these things will make us more productive. According to Covey, "Renewal is the principle—and the process—that empowers us to move on an upward spiral of growth and change, of continuous improvement...

We must never become too busy sawing to take time to sharpen the saw."

In this case, the saw is a metaphor for learning, resting, and generally taking time away from work. It may seem counterintuitive at times, but taking time out to learn, rest or exercise can often make us more productive.

And if you don't believe Stephen Covey, we can go back even further. Abraham Lincoln famously said, "Give me six hours to cut down a tree, and I will spend the first four hours sharpening the ax." Lincoln also knew the importance of taking time to prepare, learn, and rest.

As you can see, you must sharpen your saw by learning (and resting too). So, the two big questions you need to answer are:

1. What methods will you use to sharpen your saw?

2. When will you make the time to sharpen your saw?

Methods for Sharpening Your Saw?

Let's start with the different methods or vehicles you can use to invest in yourself and continuously sharpen your saw. Here are a few ideas:

Read blogs, articles, white papers, and books – There is so much content out there that with enough time (and maybe a small budget for books or content subscriptions), you can learn and become an expert on just about any subject. I love reading books on many subjects, including, and especially, business and personal development. I have already mentioned many books and will give more recommendations in the bonus section on our website.

Listen to audiobooks, podcasts, and audio classes – If you don't have much time to sit down and read, but you do have a long commute or spend a decent amount of time walking your dog, you may want to use that time productively by listening to audiobooks, podcasts, or audio classes. Almost all books now have audio versions, and there are nearly a million podcasts available with several in just about any niche you can think of. I host two podcasts *(The Talent Development Think Tank and The Andy Storch Show)* and listen to many more. Podcasts have been an important medium for me to learn from over the last ten years. There are podcasts about every subject you can think of. It is incredible what is available to you for free if you have a smartphone and podcast app (and maybe some headphones).

Take Online Courses or Watch Videos – There are thousands of online courses you can take now via many different websites, colleges, and other platforms. LinkedIn has a popular platform called "LinkedIn Learning," which came from its acquisition of Lynda.com in 2015 and holds a huge catalog of classes. And there are plenty of alternatives like Udemy, Coursera, EdX, and so many more. YouTube has tutorials on just about everything as well. If you ask people where they would go to learn how to fix something in their house, YouTube is usually their first response.

Go to our website (ownyourcareerownyourlife.com) to find out what courses we have available to reinforce your learning and take more action from this book.

Attend conferences, classes, and seminars – You can also take your online learning to the next level by attending conferences and seminars or taking classes at a college. I attend many conferences and seminars (or did before

COVID-19 hit the pause button on live events), not only learning a ton but also making great connections to grow my network in ways I otherwise couldn't (more on networking in the next chapter). You can also attend virtual conferences and summits, webinars, and even virtual networking events. I recently hosted my first virtual summit, which brought nearly 2,000 people together.

I'm also a big fan of investing in personal development, so I love seminars and programs from Tony Robbins and others who help build self-awareness, break through limiting beliefs, and live your best life. And as I sit here writing this, I can't help but reflect on the fact that the idea for this book came to me at a conference I attended in London.

Formal Education – When people want to make a big pivot in their careers or improve their resume to qualify for higher levels of leadership, the classic method has always been to go back to school and earn an advanced degree. While there are many more options out there to learn, going back to school is still a great option. And often, this can be done virtually or part-time while you continue to work to pay the bills.

However, this option probably requires the biggest investment in both time and money, so you'll want to consider your options carefully. When I was twenty-five, I felt like my career wasn't going anywhere and I needed a change. I decided traditional education was my best option, so that is when I went back to school and got my MBA. It cost me three years and $90,000, but I feel like the investment was well worth it for the things I learned, the friends I made, and what it did for my career.

There are also many hybrid and open-source platforms where you can take college classes virtually without investing a huge amount in a degree program.

Social Media – Finally, don't forget about social media. It often gets a bad rap for all the cat memes and political arguments. Many people see it as a time suck. But there are many things I like about social media, and one of them is that you get to follow and learn from experts, mentors, and masters in your field.

LinkedIn is probably the best place for this, but I also like following and learning from influencers on Instagram and Facebook. As with anything, you have to remember to take control of your experience, which means curating your content feed and intentionally looking for people or topics that will enhance your life. Find the experts or hashtags that are popular in your field and follow them on LinkedIn and other platforms. I learn stuff daily by following many experts and influencers on LinkedIn.

Start by thinking about the authors you enjoy, podcasts you listen to, or experts in your field and look them up to see if they post regular content.

If you want more advice about how to do this and how to take control and own your social media experience and not let it own you, I have created a bonus resource to help you. Go to our website and click on bonus resources.

When and How Will You Sharpen Your Saw?

You are sharpening your saw now by reading this book, but it won't matter unless you make a plan and continue to take action. There is no shortage of content or options for you to learn. But the biggest hurdle that often gets in the way is making time to do it.

I know you've got a lot going on. You are working on multiple projects; your boss keeps assigning new work, and the emails never stop coming in. Not to mention all the calls, texts, and social media notifications that hit throughout the day. Who has time for learning?

I'm right there with you. I live and work in the modern world too. The big secret I've discovered is that you've got to make time for learning. You've got to prioritize it and then put it in your schedule and protect that time.

For some people, that might be on lunch breaks or Fridays or evenings after work. I am a big fan of the morning routine, so I make time to read books every morning for about fifteen to twenty minutes as part of that routine. It's not a ton of time, but it adds up and having that protected time on my schedule has made a huge difference. I went from reading two or three books a year before scheduling time to reading twenty-five to thirty books a year with dedicated reading time. And as a result, I've learned a lot.

You can also use commute, dog-walking, or gym time to listen to podcasts and learn. I have many friends who use their long commutes to listen to audiobooks. The average American spends about an hour commuting each day (although that may change after COVID). Most of them are listening to the "morning zoo" or otherwise zoning out. Why not use that time for something productive like listening to a book, podcast, or audio course?

Start a book club with colleagues and schedule meetings where you get together to discuss learning every week. Having colleagues or friends involved adds a level of accountability that often motivates people to get things done—the same way having a personal trainer adds accountability to get to the gym.

Taking classes takes more dedication and investment of time, but it's often worth it and can be done from home. A few years ago, I decided I wanted to get into coaching and invested in an online certification course. The course work required four to five hours a week for twenty weeks. Not a ton of time but also not easy to find when you have a full-time job and a family. So, I blocked time in the afternoon three days a week to watch the classes, study, and do the homework. At the time, I had a job, so I made sure to block this time in the afternoon to get the work done for my job before the afternoon block. Then, I blocked the time, and I protected it like any other meeting so that people did not book me during that time.

That allowed me (a long-time procrastinator) to keep up with the course and finish it pretty close to on time.

Now It's Your Turn

Now it's up to you. How and when will you prioritize continuous learning? Which methods will you use (books, podcasts, courses, videos, conferences)? And when will you do it?

Take a moment to reflect and write down some ideas in your journal. Can you schedule in a daily or weekly habit to read, learn, and reflect? I promise that if you do, it will pay dividends for your career and your life. It has for me.

Old Habit: Spending all your time in reaction mode and leaving no time for learning.

New Habit: Blocking time each day or week for reading and learning to help you prepare for the future.

CHAPTER SUMMARY AND KEY TAKEAWAYS

Remember that the world is changing, nobody can predict the future, and the best thing you can do is start preparing now by doing the things that are important but not urgent, like learning new skills and building your capabilities for the future. To do this, you need to "sharpen your saw" regularly by prioritizing learning.

You can do this via reading, listening, taking online courses, going to conferences and seminars, and following gurus on social media.

There are so many options out there to learn, so you have no excuse other than time and motivation, and you can get past those by connecting with your purpose and making it a priority to learn regularly. Once you figure out how you want to learn, don't forget to prioritize and schedule it so that it gets done. And find an accountability partner if you need extra motivation.

In the next chapter, we will discuss the power of building a network.

CHAPTER NINE

BUILD YOUR NETWORK

One of the best and most powerful things you can do to help prepare for the future of work is to build your network.

Building a network might mean different things to different people, so I'll start with my definition. Building a strong network means having a significant amount of meaningful connections and relationships in different companies, places, positions, and areas of life. It means adding value and helping others regularly and having people you can call on for help or ideas when you need them. That applies to both your professional and personal life.

I think the best way to build a network is to show up, ask questions, get to know people, add value, help others, and give without expectations. When you come into a new relationship with expectations or asking for things, it is usually a turn off to the people you meet. Instead, focus on getting to know others and finding out how you can help them before asking for anything.

They say you should always try to "dig a well before you're thirsty," which means that you build the network before you need it. Many people procrastinate on this and don't spend any time building their network, and then one day, they get laid off, and the first time they reach out to people is to ask for a favor or a job. You don't want to be in a desperate situation. You probably already know that when you start by doing nice things for others, they are more likely to reciprocate and help you down the line.

Almost every job I've had (and there have been many) and businesses I've been in were because of relationships. I went back and counted. Of about twenty different job changes, only once did I get a job from applying online (via Craigslist in 2003!). Every other job and business opportunity came from someone making an introduction or referring me. That includes my very first job, which my mom got for me when I was fifteen.

You might already be good at this. But maybe you haven't done this at all because you haven't made it a priority or because you consider yourself introverted or shy. No matter where you are on this spectrum, you must make it a priority and start building your network now. Before we go into how, let me share a story.

My Networking Story

I was a pretty shy kid growing up. I always had a few core friends but never branched out much to talk to new people. I probably only had a group of about eight core friends in high school. When I got to college at the University of Florida (a school with 50,000+ students), I joined a fraternity, much to my parents' surprise, and began learning how to socialize and get to know different people. My mother recalls that I declared to her that I was going to change and stop being shy. I embraced it and ended up being elected to several positions, including chapter president, which was probably a shock to most of my family. And I'm so glad I did, because joining the fraternity and serving as president allowed me to meet many people, including my wife!

I got even more serious about networking when I enrolled in business school at the University of Southern California in 2005. I was paying a lot of money for this grad degree and was determined to get the most out of it. Luckily, I discovered and read a powerful book called *Never Eat Alone* by Keith Ferrazzi, and it opened my eyes to the importance of networking, how, and why to do it.

With that book as my guide, I went on a mission to meet as many people as possible when I started school. Right away, I met a great friend named Taiki Esheim, who was equally interested in networking, and we started a competition to see who could meet more people. That was a catalyst that led to us developing a large network and being elected to multiple positions at school.

I started meeting everyone I could and asked them questions to get to know them better. I even went as far as carpooling and getting rides and going to the gym with different people. That resulted in me building more relationships and being elected president of my class of seventy-five students that first year and eventually being elected president of the whole MBA program of about 700 students.

I'm not saying that the president of anything should be elected just because they have the biggest network. I know I have some great leadership and speaking skills as well. But let's be honest, much of life is about who you know. While I failed miserably at that game in high school, I finally figured it out in business school.

I have not let up on networking since business school. I got into consulting, started traveling more, meeting up with old friends, and meeting new friends wherever I went.

In 2017, I started my first podcast and saw how it gave me access to so many interesting people I never would've met otherwise. So, I started another podcast for talent development when I became an independent consultant. I also started attending a lot of conferences and interacting with people on LinkedIn and other social media platforms. My network continued to grow until I hosted my own conference (the Talent Development Think Tank) in January 2020.

Another catalyst has been joining mastermind groups and online communities. I first joined a mastermind group and Facebook Group for dads, where I made a lot of really great friends. I'm also involved in other masterminds and paid communities for entrepreneurs and have met so many fantastic people that I connect and talk with regularly.

Today, I still spend a considerable amount of time on networking via social media, conferences, live events, networking lunches, etc., and it continues to pay off with more great people in my network. You may not be able to dedicate as much time and money to networking as I do, but if you start to make it a priority and spend time on it consistently, I promise it will pay off.

How to Be Great at Networking

I often get asked for my advice on networking. There are many books on the subject (I already mentioned *Never Eat Alone*), and I could probably write a whole book myself. But for now, let's start with some basics.

Curiosity is Key

The first and most important thing is to be curious. One of the best and most common traits of a great leader and great networker is curiosity. That means you desire to get to know people, understand what motivates them, what they are about, and how you can help them. I think being curious and asking questions can alleviate stress for some people who consider themselves introverted, shy, or socially awkward because they don't have to be entertaining or wow people with great stories. The main thing you need to do to get to know people and get them to like you in conversations is to be curious and ask them questions.

If you've ever read the seminal classic *How to Win Friends and Influence People* by Dale Carnegie, you know that everyone's favorite subject is themselves. Even more importantly, my friend, Michael Bungay Stanier (author of *The Coaching Habit* and *The Advice Trap*), once told me in an interview that, "everyone wants to be heard."

So why not take advantage of that and ask people questions about themselves?

Of course, to have a great conversation, there needs to be some back and forth. If you only ask questions, then it turns into more of an interview. So, my rule of thumb for networking conversations (those conversations you are having with people you just met) is to get the other person to do about seventy percent of the talking. It doesn't always work out this way, but if I'm talking thirty percent of the time, I feel like the conversation is a success. Why seventy percent?

Well, there is no science behind it, but as I said, I want the other person doing most of the talking, because then, I get to learn more about them and how I can potentially help them. I have found that people like me a lot more when they do more of the talking. Dale Carnegie said the same thing in 1936, and nothing has changed. People love to talk about themselves. I'm talking about myself now!

But as I said, you want some back and forth. I have also found that if people talk about themselves too long, many will start to feel self-conscious and desire to turn the tables. So, of course, you want to be ready to contribute as well. Plus, if you don't talk, they won't know who you are or how they can help you as well.

So be curious. Ask questions. And if you need a little more help or consider yourself shy or socially awkward, I often recommend thinking of yourself as a reporter. When a reporter is interviewing someone for a story, they ask a lot of questions to learn as much as they can about the who, what, when, where and why behind something.

Some questions to consider:

- What do you want to know about the person you're talking to, and what can you uncover?
- What is challenging them?
- What is motivating them?
- What help do they need?

Think of it as your job to find out the answers!

Seeking to Help and Provide Value

The more you try to help and provide value to others, the more they will try to do the same for you. You can't and shouldn't expect anything in return, but in general, that is how life (and karma) work. It's how you build a reputation of being someone helpful (more on reputation and personal brands in the next chapter).

Of course, there are limits to this, and you can't help everyone. My first objective in any conversation, especially with a new acquaintance, is to figure out a way to help them or add value to their life. Maybe it's an introduction or recommendation, or maybe it's just listening to them or giving feedback on an idea. It could even be buying something from them or paying for a service or solution.

And if you are an entrepreneur or are in sales, offering your product or solution could be a way of helping them and providing value if it truly is something they could benefit from. But you have to be careful about leading with selling because it can turn some people off.

Often, the best thing you can do to help is give a simple recommendation to a service provider you have used. People love buying things based on recommendations and usually prefer it to buying based on searches, ads, or anonymous reviews. I do, and there is plenty of data to back that up. I always love getting good recommendations from friends and people I meet.

If you are seeking a new job or changing careers, asking for advice from someone could be a way of adding value to them. I know it seems like they are giving to you, but people love to help others, and it makes them feel good to be asked for their advice. The other day, a woman who attended my conference reached out to me to ask for some career advice. She basically said she wanted to be like me (flattery will get you everywhere) and would love to have my advice on building a network and brand that allows me to host live events. I was extremely flattered, gave her my advice, and felt great that I could help.

One caveat about giving advice is that if people ask you for help, you may not want to jump to giving advice too quickly. In his book, *The Coaching Habit*, my friend, Michael Bungay Stanier, says that most people jump too quickly to giving advice when asked for help and that the danger is that we often don't understand the underlying issue. He goes more in-depth on the subject in his next book, *The Advice Trap*, where he details how people make the mistake of giving advice and how it takes power away from the person asking for help. His advice is to stay curious longer and help the other person discover answers for themselves.

I love getting help and coaching, but I get turned off when people jump to giving me advice that I didn't ask for. When I first decided to write this book, I reached out to a respected author and speaker to share my idea.

So be careful about giving unwanted advice.

Quick Exercise

One quick exercise I have done and like to recommend others do is think back to all the jobs you've had, the classes you've taken, and any big investments you've made. Try to pinpoint why you found or got those jobs, took those classes, or made those investments. Sometimes it was simply because of an online search or ad. But if you are like me, many of them were because of personal connections, recommendations, or relationships.

And if that's not the case—if you've gotten everything yourself (applying online, etc.), you probably have not been spending enough time building your network.

Your Turn

Now it's your turn. I want you to establish some new habits and practice them regularly. Take out your journal and write down some thoughts from this chapter. Are you going to be giving more attention and spending more time building your network in the future? If so, write that commitment down and share it in our Facebook Group.

Here are your habits . . .

Old Habits: Avoiding new conversations, staying quiet, or talking too much about yourself.

New Habits: Getting really curious and learning as much as you can about people and seeking to help them first.

Practice: Look for an opportunity to meet someone new and have a conversation (networking event, phone call, etc.) or reach out to a good friend with a phone call and try to notice how much you are talking vs. listening, and see if you can shift the balance to talking about thirty percent of the time.

Networking and meeting new people can be hard and uncomfortable, but you never know where it will lead until you do it. As my friend, Ben Killoy, likes to say, "You are always just one conversation away from changing the rest of your life."

CHAPTER SUMMARY AND KEY TAKEAWAYS

Building a network is one of the most powerful and important things you can do to ensure a successful career. That's because people always prefer to hire and do business based on relationships. So, the bigger your network and the more people you know in different areas, the easier it will be to get help down the road when you have important career decisions to make.

You want to build your network before you need it (don't wait until you get laid off or want to change jobs), and to do it, you need to be proactive (spend time and money if you can) and be curious.

Ask questions and get to know others, so they feel heard. And finally, always seek to help and provide value before asking people for favors or other things. Think about karma and how what you put out into the world often comes back to you. So, if you are a giver, people will give to you. And if you are always taking from others, you can't expect others to give freely to you.

Now that you know why you need a network and the general philosophy let's get into how and where to build your network.

CHAPTER TEN

HOW AND WHERE TO BUILD YOUR NETWORK

We've covered the reasons for building a network, as well as my story and some of the mechanics of talking to people and building relationships. Now, I want to talk about how and where you can go and methods to build your network as well as how much time and money to invest.

Investing in Building Your Network

Let's start with investing. Because building your network will likely require an investment of time and money. When I went to college and joined a fraternity, there was a cost associated with it. I still remember the criticism from those who didn't join fraternities—they didn't need to "pay for their friends." And it's true. Perhaps you've said that at some point. You should never have to pay for friends, but you may want to pay for *access* to friends. It could be via groups, associations, events, masterminds, degree programs, and yes, fraternities and sororities.

I didn't pay for those friends, but I paid a membership fee to be part of a fraternity that gave me access to lots of friends. A few years later, I decided to get an MBA and chose USC Marshall School of Business partly because of proximity and ranking (I lived in LA), but primarily because the school was known for its network.

That MBA cost me $90,000 (plus interest), and more than a decade later, I can say with confidence that the most significant benefit of my investment has been the network—all the friends I made that I can still call on. Not to mention the thousands of alumni I can reach out to who would probably take a meeting with me purely because of our mutual association with the school. Perhaps you've experienced this with your school or association as well.

When I was in my final year of business school and looking for new jobs, I started reaching out to random alumni (I found via the database or LinkedIn), asking them if they would chat with me, and nearly 100% said yes.

When I invested in that degree, I was not directly paying for friends, but I joined a program and alumni association that gave me access to many people I might not have met otherwise. And the same can be said for any other groups or associations.

Today, I still invest a ton of my time and money into building my network. As I write this, I belong to two paid mastermind groups and other online groups associated with those. I also attend a lot of conferences and seminars. I hosted my own conference with my friend Bennett Phillips. All of these things cost me a lot of time and money, and they continue to help me build my network and continue to pay off with support, connections, introductions, and opportunities.

So, my question for you is, how much time or money are you investing in building your network? And is it enough? If you have not previously been investing much of either, it might be time to start. If it doesn't come naturally to you, you may need to get intentional and schedule time for it.

Okay, let's talk about where you can go to build your network. That includes:

- Networking groups and professional associations (in-person and online)
- Conferences and virtual summits
- Internally within your company
- Online via social media and membership groups
- Other misc. social outings

Where to Network: Networking Groups

One of the most traditional places to meet people and build your network is in local networking groups. I've tried many of these over the years and find them to be inconsistent. You might go to a couple and find them useful, and others are a waste of time. They are often full of real estate agents trying to sell to you, but now and then, you find a gem. So, I keep trying. I find it depends a lot on who is organizing the event, what kind of person they are, and their vibe.

I once joined a local networking group that was growing, and the host seemed like he had good intentions. But, after I got to know him, I saw a side of him I did not like, so I eventually stopped attending his events. I am still glad I went because I made a few friends there, including Tom Craig, who runs an IT Services business in Orlando and hosts regular networking lunches that attract great people. They work because Tom is a generous, caring person who organizes events purely to help people and make friends. And even after COVID hit, he kept hosting monthly virtual meetings for people to network and learn about local businesses.

That reminds me of an important thing to think about when attending networking events. Many people go, hoping or expecting to find a new client, job, or some other valuable connection. My first goal is always to make friends with the faith that those friendships will lead to great things later on.

How to Get a Conversation Started

When attending a networking event, it can often be intimidating when you walk in the room and don't know anyone. Remember my advice about getting curious? You can also use honesty and vulnerability to win people over. An example would be walking up to someone (or group of people) and saying, "I always feel awkward in these situations and never know what to say, but you look like someone I should meet." They are usually very receptive, and the conversation goes from there.

Some questions you can ask at networking events:

- How did you find out about this event?
- Why did you come?
- What kind of work do you do and how long have you been doing it?
- What do you love about the work you do?
- What is most challenging about the work you do?
- What fun things do you do when you're not working?
- Do you have a long-term goal or vision for your career? (You have one now!)
- What kind of help are you looking for?
- If I could wave a magic wand and help you achieve your goals, what would that look like?

These should help you get the conversation going. Just remember to be curious.

Where to Network: Conferences and Virtual Summits

I love conferences because they bring people together from many different places, usually with a common interest or goal. It could be an industry interest, hobby, profession, or a common goal (like grow sales or improve their lives). I think that is important because they include two vital ingredients for getting good conversations started:

1. People usually come voluntarily, which means they want to be there
2. There is a common interest, which makes it easier to start conversations

The first point isn't as important as the second. I think it's easier to start a conversation with someone excited to be in the room. Plenty of people have made friends in school or even prison by bonding over the fact that they did not want to be there. But those may not be the kind of relationships you are pursuing.

The second point is critical. The best and easiest way to get a conversation started with someone is over a common interest. If you are both attending a conference on a common topic, like HR or podcasting, or even ice skating or Star Trek, you automatically have something in common.

It is then just a matter of asking questions and having a conversation to see what other common interests you have. I once heard that a conversation is simply two (or more) people trying to find common ground. And you'll often find it easily at conferences.

As I write this, we are in the middle of a global pandemic, and there are not many in-person conferences happening. But there are a lot of virtual summits and virtual conferences popping up (I recently hosted my first). While it's not quite as easy or fun to strike up a conversation at a virtual event as it is in person, there are still plenty of opportunities to meet and connect with new people. Some virtual summits only feature presentations, but many have interactive sessions, networking events, and even an app you can take advantage of to connect and network with others.

So, what kinds of conferences should you attend?

This book is about your career, so we should probably start with professional topics like trade shows and conferences aimed at your profession. If you do a quick Google search, you'll find plenty of conferences for HR, Finance, Legal, IT,

Accounting, Insurance, Sales Professionals, and just about anything you do for a living. Some are better than others, so you'll have to ask around and read the website to see what you're getting into, but they are almost always a good investment. Often, you can get your employer to pay for it.

But don't forget about those hobby and interest conferences as well. They may be focused on hobbies, like Legos, ice skating, or games, but almost everyone there has a job or business as well, and you never know who you might meet by attending.

Conferences Cost Money!

If you don't attend many conferences, I can hear the complaints or questions now. Doesn't it cost a lot of money to attend a conference? And the answer is yes, but it's almost always worth it. Most conferences will cost $500-$1,000 for a ticket, and then you have flights and hotels. So, they are often a significant investment. And that's good because it means they only attract people who are serious about attending, and those are the kinds of people you want to meet. Lest you think I'm giving advice I don't follow, here is a list of conferences I paid money to and traveled to in the last couple of years (and most of them I attend annually):

- Podcast Movement
- Podfest Multimedia Expo
- Growth Now Movement Live (hosted by my friend, Justin Schenck)
- Social Media Marketing World in San Diego
- The Thing Live hosted by my friend, Terry Weaver
- Youpreneur Summit in London hosted by Chris Ducker
- Argyle Human Capital Forum

- Conference Board Leadership Development conference
- Total Life Freedom Mastermind Retreat
- Ascension Leadership Academy in San Diego
- Converting Corporates Workshop in London hosted by Jessica Lorimer
- The Talent Development Think Tank (my conference)

The good news about the pandemic and growth in virtual conferences is that they tend to be much cheaper for tickets and don't require travel costs.

When deciding which conferences or summits to attend, most people look at the speakers and ask themselves, "What do I want to learn?" But what I usually do is look at a conference and ask myself, "What kinds of people will be there?" Then I make my decision based on that. I often attend conferences where I've never heard of any of the speakers. So, if I learn anything from them, that's a bonus. But my main objective is to meet and build relationships with the attendees. I always advise that you look at attending conferences for the people you might meet more than what you'll learn from the speakers.

That means you need to take advantage of all the networking time while you're there. Don't skip the networking breaks and dinners or the virtual networking sessions for those online conferences. Many people take those opportunities to check email, but I'm usually moving around the room, finding someone interesting to talk to. If it helps, remind yourself that you (or your employer) paid a lot of money for you to be there, and it's a rare opportunity, so don't waste it!

Host Your Own

If you want to get crazy (like me), you can also host your own conference or small event(s). That's what I did. After attending many conferences, my friend, Bennett Phillips, and I decided to create our own.

The idea was born in February 2019 over a few conversations. Within a couple of months, we had created a website and announced it to the world. It took several more months of hard work, marketing, organizing, etc., but we made it work. In January 2020, the first Talent Development Think Tank Conference kicked off with 150 people in the room. It was a big hit.

Hosting a conference is a ton of work and not something I recommend to everyone. But you can start to organize small networking events and happy hours (I've done many of these), which helps you bring the right people together and be seen as a connector. If those go well and you have a large network, consider hosting larger events or a conference. Why not? Life is short.

Internal Networking

I've talked a lot about external sources like networking events and conferences, but if your goal is to be more successful in your career and you think there is a good chance you'll be staying with your current company for at least another six months, then you need to build an internal network as well.

Building an internal network means branching outside of your small group or team and building relationships with different people around your company. Why? Here are some reasons:

1. Having a bigger network in your company often leads to having a better understanding of how the company works, which can lead to more success in your career. Just because you work in HR or Legal doesn't mean you shouldn't understand the company strategy, financial statements, or sales process. You should. And expanding your network into those departments will help you.

2. Having more relationships around the company may make it easier to get things done. When you need budget approval or someone else to help with a project, it's a lot easier when you have a relationship and some political capital.

3. If you work for a large (or even medium) company, there will often be job opportunities that pop up in other divisions or groups, and, as with jobs in any company, they often go to people who know the hiring manager or are referred to them personally.

How do you go about building your internal network?

In normal times, you can organize lunches or happy hours in large or small groups or just meet people one-on-one for lunch or coffee. And you can always just stop by someone's desk or office and ask them some questions to see what they are working on and what else is going on in their life.

In the post-COVID virtual world we live in, you will need to be more intentional by reaching out to people to schedule conversations by phone or Zoom.

You can also seek formal mentors or more official agreements to teach each other things about what the other is working on. One of my podcast guests, Professor Jay Conger, told a great story about a woman in HR who wanted to better understand the business financials. So, she went to the company's controller and asked him to mentor her and teach her about the business for a few months. In the end, she knew all about the company finances, and it was a huge stepping-stone toward helping her excel in her career.

What if I work remotely or am not at the home office?

More and more people are working remotely or virtually for their jobs. As I write this during the COVID-19 pandemic, almost everyone I know is working remotely. That creates new challenges for internal networking but is not an excuse to avoid it. You just have to be more intentional since there are fewer opportunities to bump into someone by the coffee pot.

Start to think about the people you want to know better (peers, potential mentors, key people in other departments) and reach out to them to schedule a "virtual coffee" or phone call. With excellent video technology like Zoom, you can set up virtual coffees with colleagues and get on video for twenty minutes to chat and get to know each other. You can also schedule phone calls and small group chats and virtual happy hours. There are no limits, and I highly encourage video over a phone call because it adds a level of intimacy and connection that you can't get on the phone, although I still like doing phone calls so I can walk and talk.

Whether you work in the office or remotely, I highly encourage you to get more intentional and make time for regular conversations to build your network and new relationships around the company and outside the company.

Let's discuss your new habits and write them down.

Old Habit: Focusing on your work and assuming that doing great work is all you need to succeed in your career (spoiler alert, it's not). Spending almost no time talking with people outside of your small group or department.

New Habit: Being more intentional and going out of your way to connect with people and build your network consistently.

Ideas: To help you build the internal network, you can organize a weekly or monthly lunch or virtual coffee for groups of people. Of course, you can also reach out to people directly and ask if you can chat on the phone or Zoom. All of these things are effective for building your network and should be part of a regular habit.

Where to Network: Social Media

I mentioned earlier that social media could be a great place to learn. It's a great place to build your network as well. I have made many great friends online who became great friends in real-life as well. That has mostly been through Facebook and LinkedIn, but I know people who have made plenty of friends via Twitter and Instagram as well.

How? You can join groups (free and paid), or seek out the types of people you might like to know and start engaging with their content. Invite them to join you on a Zoom call or phone call and get to know them. I run a membership community for talent development professionals that has grown and created many great connections.

If you are looking for a great place to start, we are building a community for just this purpose.

When networking with a purpose (like finding your next job), I love leveraging LinkedIn to find people who are already doing the job you might eventually want. You can then send them a message to ask if they are interested in meeting for coffee or doing a phone call.

It's important not to seem too needy, or like you are asking for anything other than their advice. Once you find the people you might like to learn from, connect with them, and you can send them a message something like this:

"Hi Cindy, I'm pursuing a career in marketing, and I noticed you have a successful marketing career. Could we connect for a virtual coffee so I can ask you some questions about your career and maybe get your advice?"

I find most people are very open to mentoring and helping others and will say yes to this type of request.

I like Facebook groups built around shared interests for just networking in general (not looking for specific advice). In 2017, I joined a (paid) mastermind group for dads called The Dad Edge, run by my friend, Larry Hagner. I made many friends over a couple of years there, and many of them are friends I still talk with regularly.

If you are looking for a group to join where you can meet other great professionals, you can check out the Own Your Career Own Your Life Facebook Group I created for this purpose. I also recommend you search groups focused on your niche or goal. There are tons of great groups out there if you look.

By posting, sharing, and supporting content about talent development on LinkedIn, I have connected with some great people, and some of them have turned into friends in real-life who I can call for any reason. One great example is my friend Kevin M. Yates, who is a speaker on measurement in Learning and Development (L&D). We connected on LinkedIn in 2019 and started to support each other's content. Then one day, we got on the phone and hit it off. We met in person for lunch when I went to Chicago (where he lives) for client work. I ended up inviting Kevin to speak at my conference, and we have been great friends since.

If your conversation is productive and focused, you can meet many great people on social media that can turn into friends, colleagues, business partners, or even life partners.

Building a great network on social media will require you to develop a healthy habit and spend time there. Speaking of habits, remember that all social media sites and apps are designed to be addictive, so use caution and control your engagement.

To do this, you'll need to be focused on how and where you spend your social media time and not getting sucked into political discussions or cat photos (unless that helps you make friends). Start to see social media time as an important investment. Use that time wisely.

Old Habit: Avoiding social media, or only using it to follow real-life friends.

New Habit: Dedicate a certain amount of time (maybe an hour a day or week) on social media to connect with other professionals in your industry, find mentors, or make friends with those who have common interests.

Investing to Build Your Network

You may notice from all the advice and suggestions I've given in this chapter that you have to be willing to invest both time and sometimes money to build a great network.

Time

Time is your most important and limited resource. You can always make more money, but you can't get more time. Therefore, how you spend your time is critically important. If you are looking for a new job or growing your network, you will need to invest time in meeting people and building relationships. That might mean attending networking events and conferences or spending an hour or more a week connecting with people on social media.

If you are easily distracted or haven't been big on networking, attending events, or social media, you need to write down goals, schedule the habits or activities, and stick to your schedule. Some goals you may want to set that could be helpful are:

1. I will attend at least one conference and four virtual networking events this year.

2. I will network inside my organization by coordinating a lunch or virtual coffee with at least one new person each week or month.

3. I will spend at least one hour a week on LinkedIn connecting with people in my industry or who are doing jobs I may want one day.

Money

If you are serious about building your network and meeting great people, as we discussed earlier, you may need to invest some money in the process. It's not required. I've met some great people at the park or through my kids' school. But most of the people I have in my network I admire and would turn to for help, I met because I invested time and money in attending conferences, joining mastermind groups, or private online communities that require a monthly fee. Here are some ways you can invest money on networking:

1. Attending conferences or virtual summits

2. Networking groups or memberships (online and offline)

3. Private Facebook or LinkedIn groups

4. Private mastermind groups or group coaching programs

5. Using LinkedIn Premium or another premium tool to find the right people

A note about LinkedIn Premium. People often ask if it's worth it, and as with many things, the answer is, "it depends." It depends on what you are using it for. If you are in sales or you are actively looking for a job, getting LinkedIn Premium or Sales Navigator (their expensive sales tool) might be worth it if you're going to use it all the time to search for the right people to connect with and send a lot of messages. I recommend you start with the free version of LinkedIn and if you start to bump up against its limits of searches or messages, then try Premium for a month or two and see if you get value. I've been a LinkedIn Premium subscriber for many years.

Old Habit: Not making time for networking. Putting it off for someday and focusing only on the work in front of you.

New Habit: Investing time and money regularly into networking. Decide how much you can dedicate and start spending or investing money into networking regularly and see how it starts to pay off for your life and career. Note: I can't tell you exactly which groups to join or events to attend, and there is no money-back guarantee here, so spend wisely.

Your Turn

Reflecting on all we've learned about networking, take out your journal and write down some of the ways you will work on building your network. How will you take action and how often will you invest in building your network? Write those down now.

CHAPTER SUMMARY AND KEY TAKEAWAYS

We already know how important it is to build your network and that it will take both time and money. But you can't just wish it to be true. You've got to take action. You can build your network by going to local networking events, attending conferences, going to lunch or coffee with people inside your organization, or spending more time connecting with people on social media.

If you have not previously been in the habit of investing time or money into networking (or doing any networking at all), you may need to shift your mindset. Is this going to be an important investment? If so, will you dedicate a certain percentage of your budget and a few hours a week or month to building your network?

If you are looking for an easy place to start, you can:

1. Connect with me and follow me on LinkedIn (please personalize your invitation and let me know you read my book).

2. Join our Own Your Career Own Your Life Facebook Group.

3. Join our email list to find out about future live events where we can meet up and network in person! Just head over to ownyourcareerownyourlife.com to sign up.

CHAPTER ELEVEN

BUILD YOUR PROFESSIONAL BRAND

The idea of a brand used to be reserved only for companies, but lately, we realize that people have brands as well. I have been studying this idea of building a personal or professional brand for a while now, and I think it is becoming increasingly important. So, what is a personal brand, and why do you need one?

Your personal or professional brand is basically your reputation. It's what people think about you or say about you when you're not around. You want that reputation to be positive and helpful in your career.

Interestingly, you have a reputation or brand, whether you are intentional about creating it or not. Think about all of your colleagues, friends, and other people you know. If I asked you about each of them and forced you to describe them, you'd likely have some opinion. You might say, "John is nice, but he's always late to meetings," or "Madison is extremely generous and always goes out of her way to help people on projects," or "Christine is a true expert in the area of employee development, and I want to learn from her." All of those are products of the reputations or brands that those people have created, whether intentional or not.

So why do I bring this up in a book about taking ownership of your career? Because I strongly believe that in this era of work, to ~~truly own your career~~, you also need to own your professional brand and be intentional with the reputation or brand you create.

Like it or not, we all have a reputation and a brand; all you get to choose is whether you are intentional about creating it. I don't mean tricking people or being fake. I would never recommend showing up as anything other than yourself. I'm very much in favor of authenticity, vulnerability, and transparency.

Start by thinking about how you are showing up at work and how others are perceiving you. Building your personal and professional brand means being more intentional with your actions to impact your reputation. It might be how much extra work you do, how friendly and helpful you are to others, posting and chatting on internal collaboration tools like Slack, Chatter, or Yammer, or the type of work you do. It can also include how you show up on social media and other places where people can form an impression of you. I'll discuss each of these.

Why You Need a Brand

Why should you even worry about this, anyway? You get your work done, and that should be enough, right? Wrong. There are many reasons for being intentional with your brand and speaking up about your work and what you've accomplished.

First, you may have heard that the squeaky wheel gets the grease, which means that the most noticeable problems (or people) get the attention. And you may have noticed that some people tend to get rewarded more, simply because they found a tactful way to let others know what they are doing. My friend, Gemma Stow, in the UK, is a self-promotion expert for introverted female executives. I interviewed her recently, and she said that performance only accounts for about ten percent of overall success in career progression, and the rest comes from reputation, exposure, brand, and network, among other things.

That's where self-promotion comes in. Gemma says it's critical to career success for women (and everyone). There is a balance, and you don't want to go over the line and start bragging about yourself. Nobody likes that. But you do want to find ways to promote yourself and let others know what you are doing or what you've accomplished. You can't simply assume they will notice. There are too many things going on.

Second, you may hear and read a lot about the "gig economy" and how it will change the way we work. More people are (or will soon be) freelancers and consultants than ever before. But this applies to employees in large companies as well. I predict that companies will move toward more project-based work and that people will move around from project to project more often based on needs and qualifications. As a result, people will no longer sit statically in one defined career based on their college degree (those days are going away).

So, if this prophecy becomes a reality and people can move around more and take on different projects, who do you think will get the best projects and roles? The person who does the best work or the person with the best reputation? In an ideal world, people would be rewarded only for the quality of their work and nothing else. But we both know we don't live in that world, and the person with the stronger reputation will get the project.

Consider this. You need to fill a vital project role and are considering two people. Ryan is highly skilled and gets the job done, but he keeps to himself, doesn't like to collaborate, and can sometimes get irritable when he has to rely on other people for parts of a project. Then there is Harper, who is not quite as experienced or as skilled as Ryan, but she still has plenty of potential, and what she lacks in experience she makes up for in social skills. She's great at collaborating (a real team player) and has a reputation for being fun to work with.

Who would you rather hire for this role? It may come down to personal preference, but even though Ryan has more experience and skills, Harper has a better brand and reputation and is known for being fun and easy to work with. She will probably get chosen a lot more often.

By the way, I realize that while much progress has been made, there is still a lot of unconscious bias out there for hiring decisions. Too often, people still take gender, race, religion, age, and other things into consideration when making hiring decisions. I believe strongly in diversity, equity, and inclusion in the workplace and do what I can to be a better ally and help with that cause. I am not an expert in this area, but I will say one thing about it.

If you come from an underrepresented group, building a professional brand and reputation becomes even more critical.

I recently interviewed my friend Kay Fabella, a diversity, equity, and inclusion (DEI) consultant and expert. She said that if you are in a traditionally overlooked group, you need to proactively increase your visibility and be even more proactive in building your brand.

As Kay says, "When you are an 'only' in the room, you have to work even harder to step up, speak up, and advocate for yourself. If your potential employer or your future colleagues don't know what your experience is or what skills you bring to the table, nothing will change for you—or for the people from your community who come after you."

Kay advises that "As an individual from an underrepresented group, you have an even greater responsibility to your community to share your story, put your expertise out there consistently, and make yourself more visible to pave the way for others. Because change can only happen when the 'onlys' become one of many. Stepping up and showing up is how minorities can take a seat at the table and reshape the conversation."

It's unfortunate that so much unconscious bias still exists and affects how business is done. Still, I'm excited to see that progress is being made, and many companies strive to improve.

This book is about taking ownership of your career and your life and being intentional with your actions. If you are part of a group of people often overlooked or more susceptible to discrimination, all the more reason to take action and intentionally build a positive reputation or brand.

A Brand Can Help With Your Next Career Change

I mentioned two big reasons to build a professional brand or reputation. It may be the "X-factor" that helps you get a promotion or a vital role inside your company. But what about getting a new job with a different company? Can it help there too? Absolutely!

Many friends have asked me for advice on how to start preparing for a future career change. After building a network (my top priority), the next thing I tell them is the importance of building a personal or professional brand, which includes a presence on social media. Why? Because there are tons of other people qualified for the job you may want, and you need to find a way to stand out. You want to give companies a reason to hire you or even to seek you out.

When recruiters are thinking about recommending someone for a job, they will first consider that person's experience and capabilities. The first place most of them go is LinkedIn, as it's the #1 place everyone goes to connect, network, find a job, etc. Most recruiters live on LinkedIn.

But LinkedIn is not just a place to store your resume and send a few messages. Many people (including me) regularly share content on there as well, and it is very easy to look at someone's profile and go back to see what they've been sharing over the last few months or years. I've asked recruiters if they look at that stuff, and the answer has always been yes.

I recently asked my friend, Adam Posner, who runs an independent recruiting agency called NHP Talent Group, about this, and he said he loves to see people proactively sharing content to show what they know or what they're learning and that it doesn't have to be original content. If you share what you're reading or learning with a point of view, it can go a long way to building your brand.

How and Where to Build Your Brand

Earlier, I mentioned some of the big benefits of building a brand and the opportunities that might come to you within your organization (internally). These include promotion or job opportunities that you might want. Therefore, the first place to think about building your brand or reputation is in how you show up at work.

That might include when you show up to the office or meetings, what projects you take, how hard or long you work, how easy you are to work with, what skills or tools you bring to the table, how curious you are, how helpful you are, and many other factors.

The next place to think about building your brand is how you show up outside your company—at home, with friends, at conferences and networking events, and on social media.

Are you the person who sits in the corner and doesn't talk to anyone? Or are you the curious person who asks lots of questions and gets to know people? Are you the energetic, fun person who walks into the room and shares energy and enthusiasm with everyone you meet? I like to think that last one is me.

How you show up impacts your reputation and brand. While I want you to be yourself and lean into your personality and strengths, consider that you may have to push yourself to change or get out of your comfort zone if your inclination is to be closed off and quiet at networking events. It's up to you.

And finally, the last and possibly biggest place to build your brand these days is on social media. How do you show up on there? Because whether you like it or not, social media is where most people are hanging out.

I'll talk more about social media in a minute. First, let's start with something that I think is foundational to building a personal brand. Self-awareness.

Self-Awareness is Key

Self-awareness is so important. We all have strengths, weaknesses, and areas we can improve. Most people have figured out what they're not very good at, but few know their real strengths. The self-aware understand their strengths and weaknesses and then get to decide which strengths they want to leverage, grow, and showcase as well as which weaknesses they may want to improve or maybe even avoid using.

For example, some of the strengths that have helped me build a network and great reputation are my ability to build relationships and make friends easily at work, create and have fun everywhere I go, strong speaking and facilitation skills, curiosity, knowledge of business and finance, and the ability to use tools like Excel. Some weaknesses that have held me back or hurt my reputation are my lack of attention to detail, lack of focus, tendency to lose track of time, making me late for most things (it's true), and the way I often avoid work if it's something I don't want to do.

You can see how those strengths can help me, but my weaknesses can hold me back.

In my current situation, I run my own business, and I have found work that allows me to almost entirely focus on my strengths and either delegate or avoid relying on some of those weaknesses. But I still need to do some detailed work occasionally, and I need to show up on time for client meetings and the workshops I run. So, I cannot completely ignore my blind spots. If I show up late enough times, I might develop a reputation for being careless. That's not a reputation I want.

What about you? What strengths do you have that might create or influence your reputation or brand both inside and outside your organization? What are some weaknesses (or mistakes you've made) that have influenced your reputation?

Now is a good time to take out a journal and make a list. Be as honest with yourself as possible. It's about your self-awareness, not about trying to impress anyone. ~~You need to own your strengths~~ (they are yours and you are awesome) ~~and your weaknesses~~ (we all have them).

Once you have those written down, consider how they might affect your reputation at work and elsewhere. If you want to take things to the next level, you can ask some of your colleagues and friends for feedback. What are you good at, and are they ever frustrated or disappointed with you? It's hard to ask for and receive feedback like this, but this is all about self-awareness, and getting feedback is often the best way for us to improve.

Make sure you take out your journal and write down some reflections. Then let's change some habits.

Old Habit: Operating with no self-awareness and never considering your reputation or how you show up in the world. Avoiding feedback.

New Habit: Thinking regularly about how to leverage your strengths, how to improve or delegate your weaknesses, how you show up in the workplace, and how that impacts your reputation.

Leveraging Social Media to Build Your Personal Brand

As I mentioned earlier, social media is a big part of business and our society today. Most of the world uses social media regularly. You don't have to be on social media, but I think it's an important tool to build your brand. I know it has helped me immensely.

If we are talking about building a professional brand that can help you in your career, the main place you need to be is on LinkedIn. Caveat that if you are an artist or in some creative or entertainment career, then perhaps Instagram, Pinterest, or Facebook might be a better choice. But for most of us, LinkedIn should be your number one place where you hang out to build your professional brand.

I have been using LinkedIn and other social media platforms to build my personal brand for more than three years and have seen many benefits. Because I work in consulting and do a lot of training and development for large companies, I spend most of my time on LinkedIn.

LinkedIn has been around since 2003, and, for most of that time, it was a great place to connect with people, show off your work experience, and maybe find a job or client, but nothing more. However, over the last few years, LinkedIn has started to take off as a place where people can share content, network, and build their brands.

I have been on LinkedIn since 2004, but I started leveraging it to share and interact with content and build my brand in 2018 and have seen many benefits. The biggest is sharing what I'm doing, creating a reputation as an expert in my space, and getting exposure to and network with others in my space.

There are many ways to use LinkedIn and other platforms to build your brand. The first and easiest is to engage with content from other people. You can do this inside groups or on the public feed. That means following your connections and interesting people and liking and commenting on some of the posts that you see, especially those that are relevant to your area of work or expertise.

When people think about building a brand on social media, they immediately think they need to post and share their original content, but that is simply not the case. You can gain a lot of credibility and a strong network and reputation by spending time leaving thoughtful comments on others' posts.

But when you are ready to start posting and sharing content, there are quite a few things you can do.

What Type of Content to Share?

When you are ready to start sharing content on social media (and if you want to build a brand, I highly encourage you to start), there are many things you can do.

Articles and Content You've Read or Consumed – Many people feel pressure to come up with their original content, but you can start and still build a great reputation and brand by sharing other people's content. It could include articles you've read, videos you've watched, or posts from people you follow. It doesn't need to be complicated. If you are following my advice and investing time in continuous learning, that means you are consuming content (articles, books, videos, courses) regularly. So next time you read an interesting article hit the "share" button and then add a little bit of commentary. Something like, "Just read this interesting article about X. I thought the author was spot on when she said xyz," or something like that.

If you find an article, video, or something else valuable, then you are simply being helpful to others by sharing it. And what you are projecting (without saying it) is that you are someone who reads and learns regularly, and others will start to see you as knowledgeable on the subject.

Start a Podcast or Blog – This is a lot more work, but if you feel like you have a lot of good content to share or you enjoy interviewing experts about a certain subject, you could start a blog or podcast to share regularly. Remember that you don't have to be an expert to start a blog or podcast, and the barrier to entry is extremely low. All you need is some basic equipment to get started. And if you do an interview-based show or blog, you can also leverage it to build your network as well. That has worked well for me. I started my first podcast in 2017 and have built a great network and found my voice as a result.

If you are looking for more advice on leveraging your content or platform to build your network, I recommend you check out the book *Content-Based Networking* by my friend, James Carbary. In it, he lays out exactly how to leverage a podcast, blog, or YouTube channel to connect with influential people and potential clients, which is exactly what I've done with my podcasts.

Conduct Interviews for a Book, White Paper, Podcast, etc. – As I already mentioned, conducting interviews for a podcast or other content is a great way to build your network and connect with experts and other influential people. Another big benefit is that by interviewing experts and sharing that content, you will be linked to those experts and seen as an expert yourself. That's what happened to me.

I launched my Talent Development Hot Seat podcast in 2018, and since then, I've interviewed dozens of experts on the subject, and as a result, many people often refer to me as an expert as well. But you don't need to produce a regular podcast. You could conduct interviews for a white paper, research project, e-book, or book and then share the results later to build your brand. And the great thing is that it does not require you to be a subject matter expert. You are simply interviewing experts and then summarizing your findings (something great authors have been doing for decades).

Share Original Content – Once you decide that you also have something to say or contribute, you can start sharing your original content. It can include text posts, solo podcast episodes, blog posts, videos, articles, etc. As I mentioned, I started my first podcast in 2018, and for a long time, all I did was interview other people and shared that. But eventually, I started sharing some of my own expertise, which turned into daily posts on LinkedIn, Instagram, and Facebook, as well as podcast episodes and articles, and finally, this book. You can start with text posts or pictures on Instagram, and if you're comfortable making and sharing videos, those can often be engaging on all of those platforms as well.

Book Reviews – This is not done very often, but I think it could be a great way to share interesting and valuable content that easily builds your brand. If you are someone (like me) who reads books regularly, you could post a short review every time you finish a book. All you have to do is say, "I just finished reading the book *Own Your Career, Own Your Life*, and I really enjoyed it and here's why I think you might enjoy reading it too . . ."

This idea was inspired by my friend, John Hernandez, who is a talent development executive and great career coach. In my eyes, John has modeled this journey beautifully. In 2019, he started out sharing other people's content (including mine) on LinkedIn and adding his own spin. He was the first person I saw share a book review. Then he shared his first article on LinkedIn and started writing more. I just checked his content recently, and he has written and posted several articles with lots of great reactions and comments. I highly recommend you find and follow him on LinkedIn.

By the way, I'd be grateful if you shared a post about this book, but you can do this with all books you read. And much like with sharing articles, you are helping others (people love a good book recommendation) and projecting that you are someone who reads regularly, which makes you look good.

Some Tips for Sharing Great Content:

1. Focus on what will provide tremendous value to others, not what will make you look good. Building your reputation and brand is the byproduct that comes from sharing great content that helps others.

2. In general, the three ways you can provide value to others on social media are to entertain, educate, or inspire. So, either you are entertaining them (could be something funny or enjoyable), educating them with interesting facts they can use, or inspiring them with things you've learned or done that might help them. I share content in all three areas, but most of my content falls in the "inspiration" bucket. You can decide where this book falls.

3. Don't feel like it has to be perfect. You are simply sharing stories, articles, and your point of view on things. Most people don't expect perfection on social media. I've made plenty of mistakes (spelling, grammar, poorly edited videos, etc.) over the years, and nobody has held

it against me. It's better to have imperfect content than no content at all.

4. Think about your target reader or consumer. There are billions of people out there and probably a couple thousand in your network who might see your content. Remember that you really can't create something that would be interesting to everyone. Instead, you need to focus on one target market, niche, or consumer and try not to worry about the rest. My Talent Development Hot Seat podcast and much of the content I share on LinkedIn is aimed at HR and Talent Development professionals. That means there are a lot of people who would not be interested or benefit, and that's okay. The content is not for them.

5. Try not to worry about judgment. The biggest thing that holds people back from sharing content on social media is the fear of others' judgment. It's that fear that you will post something, and then someone in your network (or even worse, your family or your church) will see it and roll their eyes or criticize you. But you can't worry about that because you can't please everyone. And if someone is going to see your content and judge you for it, they are not a very good friend and probably shouldn't be in your network anyway. And believe me, I've dealt with plenty of this. I know this book has the potential to help thousands of people, and I also know there will be a few people who read this book, think it's terrible, and make critical comments or leave one-star reviews. I have to be okay with that because this book is not for everyone.

Your Turn

Now would be an excellent time to take out a journal and write down some ideas you have for content and things you can do on social media to build your reputation and brand. Now is also a good time to develop new, healthy habits.

Old Habit: Avoiding social media or consuming content and never sharing your own due to fear or the limiting belief that you have nothing interesting to say.

New Habit: Spending more intentional time on LinkedIn or other social media channels. Leaving thoughtful comments on posts, sharing articles and books you've read (like this one), and starting to share some of your original content to build your brand.

CHAPTER SUMMARY

Besides building a network and relationships, one of the best things you can do to prepare for future career changes and the future of work is to build a personal brand and get intentional about the reputation you are creating (and thus others' perception of you).

That means how you show up at work, the types of projects you work on, how you leverage your strengths and improve or avoid your weaknesses. It's also significantly impacted by how you show up on social media.

Self-awareness is essential here. The more you understand yourself, your strengths, weaknesses, what energizes you, and where you can help people, the more you can share confidently and build your professional brand.

You can build your brand and reputation on social media by sharing all kinds of content, including articles and books you've been reading, courses you've taken, or your original content, including blogs, podcasts, articles, videos, and text posts.

And don't forget that you can also build your brand and network by regularly taking time to interact with others' content, and you may never need to create and share your own.

If you have questions or would like to start practicing your social media sharing, join our Own Your Career Own Your Life Facebook community.

PART III

Own Your Life

So far, we have covered how to take ownership of your career and plan for the future of your career and work, whatever that may be. There is one more critical component that we have not yet discussed, and that is taking ownership of your life.

For most of history, people were able to keep their work and personal lives separate, but that's getting harder as everything becomes more integrated, and people do more and more work from home. That was accelerated by the COVID-19 pandemic, which forced many more people to start working from home, often causing people to work more.

Work is important, but it's not everything. We have other interests and obligations. To be in control and live your life with fulfillment and happiness, I believe strongly that you need to take ownership of your life and live with intention.

But what does it mean to own your life? Doesn't everyone own their lives? We are lucky to live in a time when most people in the world today have the freedom to say and do what they like (within the confines of the law). So why do we need to discuss this?

Because the truth is, even though most of us technically have free will (the power and ability to act at our own discretion), a high percentage of people are not exercising it. Many people are drifting through life doing whatever society tells them to do or what they think they are supposed to do. They never take much time to think about how they'd like to live their lives, and even fewer people take action on that. Instead, most people spend their time doing mindless things that don't add much value to their lives.

I'm not here to judge you or anyone for how you live your life because it is your choice. My goal is to inspire you to think more about how you are spending your time and living your life and what changes you could make to find even more fulfillment.

My goal for this section is to raise your awareness and help you start to be more intentional with your actions and how they fit in with your dreams, goals, values, and purpose. By doing so, I believe you will be happier and more fulfilled. You may already be pretty satisfied with your life, but if you have even an inkling of a thought in the back of your mind that life could be better (like I did a few years ago), then this section is for you. Let's begin.

CHAPTER TWELVE

STOP DRIFTING AND TAKE COMMAND OF YOUR LIFE

Before we begin, I need to acknowledge that everyone is on their own journey with different lives and situations. We live in different places, have different families, friends, personalities, jobs, careers, businesses, genetics, health considerations and challenges. We all have different desires and goals. But regardless, we all have the power to take ownership of our lives, live with intention, be grateful and kind and, stop drifting, and take control of our futures.

I'll start by saying I've had a privileged life. No major challenges compared with others. But looking back, I spent much of my twenties doing things that didn't add a lot of value or help me grow and fulfill my true potential. For example, I was watching a lot of sports—baseball in particular. I felt like it was a necessary outlet and something I enjoyed, but looking back, it was like drinking soda—empty calories that add no value to your life.

I was always ambitious and knew I wanted more. But, for a long time, I had no idea what that meant or how to get there. I wasn't putting in the extra work. Even though I was great at networking and had many friends, I often felt helpless—like other people had things figured out, but I did not. In my mind, all of those friends were more successful than I was (we'll discuss comparison later in this section).

Fast forward to 2015. I was married with a daughter and another child on the way, and a pretty good career making six figures as a consultant that allowed me to travel all over the US and the world. And I had a lot of friends.

On the surface, it seemed like my life was great. And it's not like I was depressed or unhappy. I almost always had a smile on my face and had fun everywhere I went. Yet something was nagging at me. My life was great, but I knew I wanted more, and I had the potential to accomplish more. But I didn't know what that meant. I was also starting to get more intentional with my time (watching less sports and TV in general), but I wasn't quite sure where that was going.

As I mentioned earlier, the turning point came in January 2016 when I read *The Miracle Morning* by Hal Elrod. I had never read anything related to personal development or self-help before, but I knew I needed to read that book. It sparked something inside of me that I didn't know was there before. I hope that this book will do the same for you.

The Miracle Morning led me to invest more time in reading, learning, and self-reflection. I also started getting into meditation, mindfulness, affirmations, and entrepreneurship. I even attended Hal's Best Year Ever Blueprint conference in San Diego, my first personal development conference or event. That led me to join my first mastermind group as part of a dads' group called The Dads Edge Alliance hosted by Larry Hagner. It also led me to launch my first podcast, *The Entrepreneur Hot Seat*, in May 2017. As I continued to invest more and grow more, it opened up my world to many opportunities. I joined a mastermind group hosted by Vincent Pugliese, who became a mentor and close friend after I read his book, *Freelance to Freedom* and interviewed him on my podcast. His mastermind group and Total Life Freedom community have been instrumental in my success.

Along that journey, I learned about this concept of drift from Dominick Quartuccio, who wrote a book called *Design Your Future: 3 Simple Steps to Stop Drifting and Take Command of Your Life* (the basis for the title of this chapter).

I heard Dominick being interviewed on a couple of podcasts and eventually interviewed him for my podcasts then read his book, which I highly recommend.

Because of those interviews with Dominick, I discovered another important book called *Outwitting the Devil* by Napoleon Hill. You may already be familiar with Hill from his classic book *Think and Grow Rich*, which is the most popular and bestselling personal development book of all time.

Outwitting the Devil

Hill wrote *Outwitting the Devil* in 1938, a year after he published *Think and Grow Rich*. But because he and his wife considered the book to be too controversial, it was not published until 2011, long after their deaths.

In the book, Hill recounts a heated conversation between himself and the devil and uses it to explain the most common ways that people are drifting and the differences between drifters and non-drifters. Even though the book was written more than eighty years before I read it, I found most of it still rings true today.

In the book, the devil says that people who do not think for themselves are drifting. Drifters, he says, operate more out of fear, while thinkers, those in control, operate more out of faith. To attain mental, spiritual, and physical freedom, we must take control of our lives and stop doing things out of fear or just because we think that's what society wants us to do.

Dominick also discusses this idea of drift in his book and his interview on my podcast.

Avoiding Drift

According to both of the authors I mentioned, drift is the enemy of an intentional life. It happens when we conform to society, don't design our life or future, and just do the things we think we are supposed to do without giving them much thought.

That could include smoking, drinking too much, watching too much TV (Netflix, sports, etc.), mindlessly scrolling through social media or other content on your phone, watching cable news, excessive unhealthy eating, not taking care of your health, spending time with negative people, judging others excessively, and much more.

According to Quartuccio (and Hill), you might also be drifting if you consistently let your fears dictate your behaviors, lack the drive to make things happen, always judge or criticize others, or lack a sense of purpose in your life.

I won't go into a ton of detail about what it means to be drifting and how to take control because you can read more about it in the two books I mentioned. My point is that many people are drifting and not living their lives with purpose.

This concept resonated with me, partly because I know I had been drifting in many areas of my life, and now, I see so many others drifting. I want to help more people wake up, take control, live their lives intentionally, and fulfill their true potential. And I want to start with you.

My question for you is, where are you drifting in your life? What things are you doing just because it is the social norm or without giving much thought to how it's impacting your life? Where are you letting fear dictate your life?

I did things that I have since eliminated. I spent a lot of time watching and reading about sports. I played fantasy football, followed the news closely, drank excessively, worked jobs that didn't align with my goals, ignored my wife's needs, judged others, and didn't live my life with intention, to name a few.

From age fifteen to thirty, I probably spent over ten hours a week watching sports. Now, when I look back on it, I shake my head and wonder why. Yes, it was entertaining and certainly not uncommon. But it didn't benefit me in any way. I also worked many jobs that didn't help me progress toward any particular goal. I was not fulfilled and didn't know what to do about it. I was drifting in many areas of my life.

If you are honest with yourself, there are probably areas where you are drifting or not using your time wisely as well. What are they and should you make changes?

You are Responsible for Your Success and Happiness

As I've said before, the biggest step you can take toward making positive life changes is to become self-aware. Whether you are trying to get into better shape, end an addiction to drugs or alcohol, or stop wasting your time with mindless stuff, it always starts with the realization that you may need to make a change.

One of the most significant realizations I share with others is that we are all responsible for our success and happiness. That may seem obvious, and yet most people still let others dictate their lives. And I don't think that's a good way to go.

Over time, I have realized that you can only reach true happiness when you take full responsibility for your life. That means you never blame anyone else for your challenges, and you realize that nobody cares more about your success than you do. And therefore, your happiness starts with you.

Are you taking full responsibility for your life, success, and happiness? Are you intentional about taking action toward your goals? Do you have a purpose? Where have you been waiting for permission instead of taking action? Where have you put off things you wanted to do because of fear?

Here are a few habits I want you to engage in to take full ownership of your life:

Old Habits: Drifting, living in fear, complaining, acting like a victim, wasting time, waiting for permission or direction from others.

New Habits: No complaining, taking action on dreams and goals, not waiting for permission (unless it is necessary), and avoiding excuses.

CHAPTER SUMMARY:

Many people in life are drifting. They let society dictate how they live their lives and participate in activities that don't add much value or help them achieve their goals. But you can take control, follow your dreams, and achieve your goals.

The most crucial step is to take full responsibility for your life, fulfillment, and happiness. To do this, you need to become self-aware of who you are, who you want to be, and how you are spending your time. Then see if how you spend your time matches your goals and values. Focus your time and energy on the things that are in your control and try to worry less about the things outside of your control.

CHAPTER THIRTEEN

MINDSET IS EVERYTHING

In the last chapter, I talked about the importance of getting intentional, avoiding drift, and mentioned advice from some amazing authors and mentors I've had. When I think about all of the best advice and lessons I've learned over the years about achieving goals and living my best life, it has almost always come down to mindset. Your mindset has a heavy influence on your outlook on life, and that outlook influences your successes and failures or how you perceive your experiences.

One of the most significant shifts you can make is your belief about whether life is happening *to* you or *for* you. When you believe life happens *to* you, you assume you have no control. You believe everything is random, and you are a victim of circumstances. And while it is true many things in life are out of your control, many things are well within your control. The more you focus on what you control and believe that life is happening *for* you, the more you take ownership of your life.

Old belief: Life happens *to* me. I have no control.

New belief: Everything in life happens *for* me. I am in control.

If this is a new concept to you, then operating with this mindset will take some practice. There will always be challenges in life and things that happen outside of your control, from something as small as a traffic jam that makes you late, to economic downturns and global pandemics, to loved ones who get sick or pass away. Many of these things are outside your control. But what is always within your control is your mindset—your outlook and how you interpret life.

The best and most beloved book on this subject is *Man's Search for Meaning* by Viktor Frankl. It's about his time in a concentration camp and how he used a positive mindset to survive all the tragedy around him.

Focus on What's in Your Control

Your mindset is the foundation for taking ownership and living a great life. One of the key elements is to focus more energy on the things under your control and stop worrying so much about the things that aren't.

It starts with realizing what's in your control and what is not. If you work for a big company, your tasks are probably in your control, but the company laying people off is not.

If you think your company might lay people off, you can't control it. But you can start preparing by cleaning up your resume, networking, building your personal brand, and doing the other things in this book. Focus your energy there.

As I mentioned, there will always be challenges in life, and most of them will be outside of our control. But I find that if I spend more of my energy focused on the things in my control and accept the things outside of my control, I'm usually happier.

There is a ton of advice out there about handling challenges and things that don't go our way. One of my favorites is from Hal Elrod in his book, *The Miracle Equation*. Hal talks about the "five-minute rule" and how he set a timer and gave himself exactly five minutes to embrace and express negative emotions when things didn't go his way. After the time was up, he had to move on. He would say, "Can't change it," and acknowledged that if he can't change something, there is no point in resisting it. He says that after many times doing this, he built up emotional resilience and needed less and less time to move past challenges.

I have not been as structured (by using a timer), but I have practiced something similar and found that I have also gotten more emotionally resilient. I used to get upset about the smallest things, and now it takes a lot to get me upset (meditation has also helped).

One of the most profound lessons that Hal shares in that book is that "It's not the experience, circumstances, or event that causes emotional pain, but rather our unwillingness to accept life as it is and move forward that is the cause." And when you think about it, he is so right. By the way, if you are working on any big goals (like changing careers), I highly recommend that book.

Handling Challenges

One thing I try to do is laugh at the small stuff (like a spilled drink or broken dish). And when big challenges come up, I ask myself three important questions that put me back in control:

1. What's great about this?
2. What does this make possible?
3. What did I learn from this so I can improve next time?

These questions can be utilized in almost every challenging situation. There are some situations more challenging than others. Let's take a look at some examples.

When things are not going your way, asking, "What's great about this?" seems counterintuitive. At first glance, there may be nothing extraordinary about the situation. But almost all bad situations have a silver lining. Sometimes it is difficult to see, but it's almost always there.

Sometimes that silver lining increases awareness, a chance to connect with others, or a new beginning. It's amazing what opens up to you in life when you start looking for the silver linings.

As mentioned earlier, your outlook determines a lot of your life. If you believe that bad things always happen to you, it's often how life will play out. Conversely, if you believe that things always work out for you no matter the challenge, that is probably what will happen. Henry Ford famously said, "Whether you believe you can or you can't, you are right." I strongly agree.

So how does this apply?

During the COVID-19 pandemic, I started a habit of asking people about their silver linings. I heard so many people talk about having more time with family, getting more done around the house, increased communication with their teams, and many other benefits that came out of an otherwise lousy situation.

When I was organizing my first conference, the Talent Development Think Tank, with my friend Bennett Phillips, we planned it for November 2019 in Santa Rosa, California. We marketed like crazy, and by October, we had sold out. We were ecstatic. We had no idea if we could pull this off and worked our butts off for eight months and had achieved our goal of selling over a hundred tickets. We filled our space. Then wildfires started raging in the area and moved into the town of Santa Rosa, where our conference was going to be held. Our hotel was evacuated, and one week before the conference, we were forced to postpone. It was a tough situation.

I immediately asked the first of those three questions, "What's great about this?" I even talked about it on my podcast and LinkedIn because I wanted others to see our mindset and shift theirs as well.

The answer was that it gave us more time to plan. It allowed us to move into a bigger space on our new dates in January, and it allowed us to potentially sell more tickets.

While we lost some people who couldn't make the new dates, we kept all of our speakers and sold tickets to some new people who couldn't make it in November. Those sales included two people who would go on to become big corporate clients. I don't know if that would've happened if they didn't come to that first Think Tank.

So, while I don't know if things always happen for a reason (as many people say) I'm strongly in favor of believing it. Because when you focus on what's within your control, worry less about what's not, and look for the silver lining in every situation, things usually work out.

Since this is a career book, I want to make sure I give a good example in the career space. Let's say you lose your job, your boss leaves the company, or you miss a promotion. That question absolutely applies and is highly useful. As I write this during COVID-19, I know several people who have been laid off.

It's a tough situation, but you can always ask the questions. What's great about this? Have you been thinking about getting a new job anyway? Do you need to shake things up in your life? I've seen many friends lose jobs over the years, and though it was devastating at the moment, they almost always went on to bigger and better things.

And this relates closely to the next question, which I love to ask. "What does this make possible?"

The essence of this question is that all challenges create opportunities. If someone cancels a meeting with you, it opens up time for you to do something else you wouldn't have done otherwise. If a project at work is defunded, that creates an opportunity for you to work on something else. If a global pandemic cancels all of your current initiatives, that might create space to work on projects you've been putting off. If you suddenly lose your job, as unfortunate as it may seem, that always creates an opportunity for you to find a new one.

As I said earlier, when my conference got postponed because of wildfires that were outside of our control, we didn't waste time worrying about it. We simply asked those questions. And though it was stressful, the wildfires made it possible for us to open up more space and sell those additional tickets.

When COVID-19 hit in March 2020, it shut down a lot of my business, but I started to ask those questions and quickly found that what was great and what it made possible was that it forced me to pivot and create a new business that I love, and it allowed me to spend more time with my family.

What about you? What is something challenging that has happened in your life lately? Or what is something challenging that you are dealing with right now? Have you tried answering those questions?

The final question is, "What can I learn from this?" It's a great question to ask after mistakes or failures. I find we can learn something from almost every situation in life. Even when things happen outside of our control, and we don't think are our responsibility, we can often find a way to improve for next time.

So, if you make a mistake and screw something up at work, what can you learn? Maybe you need to pay more attention to details or ask for help. If your client cuts the budget and cancels some important work (as has happened to me), what can you learn? That your client base or portfolio needs to be diversified, so when one client cuts back, you still have other work and thus income. When your boss hands you extra work even though your workload is already full and causes you to work a lot of extra hours, what can you learn from that? Maybe you could communicate better with your boss and let them know what you are working on and how much time you have. Or maybe you learn that you don't enjoy the work and should be seeking something else to do. There are always things we can learn from every situation.

The interesting thing is that as you get more into the habit of asking the questions, you realize that you can learn something from almost every situation. You have always been learning subconsciously, and now you can be more intentional about your learning and what to do with it.

Your Turn

Now it's your turn. Where can you benefit from asking the above questions? What challenges have come up recently that you can learn from? What lessons can you learn? Can you shift your mindset from thinking of things as tragedies or failures and turn them into challenges and learning opportunities?

Old Habit: Getting upset, complaining, and otherwise spending a lot of energy resisting things that are outside of your control.

New Habit: Recognizing the things that are within your control. Setting a timer (if necessary) when bad or challenging things happen and then asking one or all of the three questions above and moving on.

Practice: Here's a good way to start practicing this now. Take out a journal and think of something that happened lately that did not go as planned for you or that you were disappointed about and then write out the answers to the three questions:

1. What's great about this?

2. What does this make possible?

3. What can I learn from this?

Growth Happens on the Other Side of Discomfort

They say that growth happens on the other side of discomfort. That means that you have to be willing to get outside of your comfort zone if you want to grow and achieve big goals. Rarely do you hear about someone achieving something big without them taking some chances, getting uncomfortable, and risking failure.

Yes, you can achieve some measure of success (money, title, etc.) by staying the course and incrementally improving in the same field. That is possible, and I'm not trying to say you need to go skydiving or completely change careers just to get uncomfortable. But I find that when we try new or scary things or attempt big goals that make us uncomfortable, those experiences are often the most fulfilling.

When I interviewed Whitney Johnson, author of the book *Disrupt Yourself*, she said it's critical that we continuously disrupt ourselves in our careers, which means we change things up every few years to get out of our comfort zones and learn new things. Otherwise, we get complacent and bored.

In 2011, I left my job as a product manager in LA for a new consulting job in San Francisco. I had never worked as a consultant and had no idea if I could do the job, even though I had performed well in the interviews and case study they gave me.

I'm sure you've been in this situation before—changing jobs and maybe even moving cities. You think it's a great opportunity, but you have no idea if you'll be successful. What if you aren't any good at the job and end up getting fired? I certainly had those questions in my mind, but I knew I needed a change. I was unhappy in my job and was getting bored with LA. I was ready for a change and ready to finally have a job that leveraged my strengths.

As I write this nearly ten years later, I have no idea if I was "successful." It turned out that I didn't quite have the right skills to move up the ranks as a consultant. There were long nights and hard conversations, and even though I worked there for seven years, I was never promoted for the reasons I explained earlier.

So, I didn't move up to become a partner and achieve success like I had hoped when I started, but I am happy I took that job. I got to try new things, learn a ton about business as well as consulting, working with clients, talent development, etc. I also made lots of new friends, built my network, and gained a ton of amazing experiences (and got to travel all over the world). I got to live in San Francisco (one of the most beautiful and amazing cities in the world) for four years. I am so glad I took that chance.

I'm sure you've had some of these experiences as well—where you tried something new (job, move, relationship, sports, etc.) that was outside your comfort zone. Maybe you didn't achieve the success you wanted (promotion, mastering the skill, winning the game, etc.), but you learned and grew from the experience. That's what life is about—the journey.

Life is About the Journey

It's often scary to try new things. It takes courage. We don't like to fail. We are afraid it will define us. We are afraid it will hurt our career, social status, or chances of achieving big goals.

But what if life is not about achieving goals at all? What if life is really all about the journey?

It might help you to stop and think about what success and failure even mean to you because they can mean different things to different people.

Like many people, I spent much of my earlier career chasing success and avoiding failure, when I never even stopped to define either one.

During those years, if you had forced me to define success, I probably would've mumbled something about making a lot of money, having a big title, achieving goals, earning admiration and respect, and maybe having the freedom to live life however you want. I was focused mostly on how to get promoted, move up, get a big title, and make a lot of money. And there was nothing wrong with that, so long as those things were aligned with my purpose, values, and long-term vision. But I didn't know what those were, which is a big reason why I'm writing this book.

Back to success. The interesting thing is that there are a lot of trade-offs in success and what we want to achieve. Having a big title and making a lot of money often go hand-in-hand, but they are hard to achieve and maintain and often conflict with the goal of freedom to live life how you want. There may be a few people who have figured out how to have it all, but I've been working in the corporate space for more than a decade, and my experience is that most senior executives who have the big title and salary are stressed, overworked, and don't get much time off.

There is nothing wrong with focusing on your career, getting promoted, working seventy hours a week and having a goal to be CEO. There are a lot of rewards that come with achieving that goal. My point is simply that if you are someone who values freedom or sees success as being able to live life how you want, this lifestyle may not match up. And at some point, you may have to choose. Would you rather work all the time and make a lot of money, or work less and make less? Not that you can't have both, but that is a common tradeoff in the corporate world.

Then there is the question of the type of work and whether it's something you enjoy. There are so many factors.

So, what then, is success? How do we define it, and how do we measure it? The technical definition of success is "the accomplishment of an aim or purpose." But how do you know if you are successful?

I have learned over time that the definition of success is very personal. It is different for everyone. For one person, success might be about money or title; for another, it's about freedom or time. For others, it might be about respect, admiration, fulfillment, or love.

And what is failure?

I define failure as not achieving the results you wanted or expected.

I spent much of my life being afraid of rejection and failure. So many people out there avoid taking chances or trying new things because they are afraid of failure. Why? Really, it's because they are afraid of the judgment of others if they fail. But when you reframe failure and stop thinking of yourself as a failure and think of failure only as something that didn't go as planned, it doesn't sound so bad.

The problem is that most people think that if they fail at something, they will be defined as a failure. That's why we need the reframe it so that we can continue to try new things. A lesson I learned from Hal Elrod is that there is no such thing as failure—only learning and growth.

I can tell you that I've achieved many goals and fallen short of many others. I try to learn from each one and keep moving forward, enjoying the journey as much as I can. When I fall short of a goal, I no longer look at that as a failure, but rather an opportunity to learn and improve for next time. And when I achieve my goals, I try to learn from that too. But I never stop growing.

Even if I achieved all of my goals and made way more money than I needed, I would probably keep building businesses, growing influence, and trying new things because it's what fulfills me.

I need to learn and grow, and I want to continue that journey.

You might be different. We all are. But I want you to think about what fulfills you and lights you up. What part of the journey do you enjoy? If you look back and find you enjoyed the struggle to achieve new or big goals, why do you shy away from taking risks?

If you make life more about the journey than actually achieving the goals, it becomes easier to take risks and try new things.

Fixed vs. Growth Mindset

Understanding the concept of having a fixed vs. growth mindset is an essential component of this.

In her 2006 book, *Mindset: The New Psychology of Success*, Dr. Carol Dweck introduced the idea that most people have one of two types of mindsets, depending on their background and beliefs—Fixed or Growth Mindset.

The first set of people she discusses has a fixed mindset, which means that intelligence and other abilities are fixed and that they either have the ability to be good at something or don't. These individuals often operate under the belief that people are smart or not smart, creative or not creative, athletic or not athletic, depending on innate abilities. For those with a fixed mindset, life is more binary, and the main focus is on ability. If you do well on a project, you are good at that type of work, and if you perform poorly on a project, you aren't good at that type of work.

The second set of people have a growth mindset, which means they have a core belief that they can always grow and get better. These people often enjoy challenges because they believe that facing challenging situations will help them grow. So, someone with a growth mindset will care more about learning and growth than being good at any one thing. They care more about improvement than results.

In the book, Dr. Dweck shares examples from business, athletics, and parenting that are very compelling. The gist is that people with a growth mindset tend to work harder to improve, enjoy the work they do more, and often achieve more success.

That is not to say that people with a fixed mindset cannot be successful. Dr. Dweck shares examples of some famous athletes and musicians who achieved success despite a fixed mindset. She also explains that many of them were constantly stressed over making mistakes because, with a fixed mindset, they worried that those mistakes would define them.

Reading this book had a profound effect on me. As I reflect on my own life, I think I spent much of my life with a fixed mindset. During my childhood, I focused on getting good grades and always worried about how it would reflect on me if I didn't. I achieved some success as a result of this focus. Thanks to pressure and guidance from my parents and the generous program in Florida (where I grew up), I received a full academic scholarship to the only college I wanted to attend, The University of Florida. But I was also often stressed about it and felt that it defined my success (or failure). That type of mindset stayed with me for many years, and I lived most of my life afraid of failure. That fear constantly held me back from trying new things. Can you relate?

I was already making big changes by the time I read that book, and it shifted my mindset. I no longer worry so much about failing when I try new things. Instead, I worry more about the regrets of not fulfilling my true potential. So, I now dive into new endeavors with less fear of failure.

It also changed how I talk to my kids. The easiest way to explain it is that I try to focus more on rewarding effort over results. Instead of congratulating them for achieving goals or winning contests or awards, I try to give more praise for working hard and trying to do something even when it seems really difficult or challenging.

The gist is that children crave attention from their parents. And when we praise results (instead of effort), they get fixated on achieving great results. If they can't, then they are likely to quit faster. So, if a kid is playing a sport and doesn't achieve success, she might worry about disappointing her parents and quit. Whereas if we as parents praise effort (over results), the child learns that hard work is more important than winning.

When my kids engage in competitive things, I ask two questions: "Did you work hard?" and "Did you have fun?" Because what's the point of life if we aren't enjoying it?

Can you see how this relates to our careers and lives as well? Take a moment and reflect on your own life. Have you felt more fulfillment when you were effortlessly good at something or worked hard to achieve something, even if you weren't the best? I get more fulfillment from growth.

If you want to learn more about this, there are tons of resources available.

CHAPTER SUMMARY

Your mindset is so important and goes a long way toward determining your happiness, fulfillment, and success. If you believe you cannot succeed, you will probably be right. And if you believe that the world is amazing and beautiful and that you have everything you need to be successful, you are still probably going to be right.

You get to choose whether you are going to take ownership and work for life to happen *for* you or if you are going to be a victim and wait for life to happen *to* you.

You also get to choose how you respond to challenges when they come up. Don't forget the three questions we discussed:

1. What's great about this?

2. What does this make possible?

3. What can I learn from this?

Even though we spent the first part of this book talking about setting a vision and big goals, remember that life is about the journey. Whether you achieve those goals or not, the most important thing is how you live your life along the journey to get where you are going. And your mindset will determine how much you enjoy that journey.

According to the book *Mindset: The New Psychology of Success* by Dr. Carol Dweck, people often live with either a "fixed" or "growth" mindset, which will determine how much effort they put into things and how much they enjoy them. I made a major shift in my mindset as a result of reading this book, and it has affected how I run my business and how I parent my kids.

You can live your life however you like. I am not here to tell you how. But if you have previously operated with more of a fixed mindset like me, I highly recommend you check out that book and think about making some changes.

So, if you are on board with all of this, now is the time to establish some new habits.

Old Habit: Avoiding risks, fearing failure or rejection, never trying new things.

New Habit: Embracing change, taking more risks, trying new things, and getting outside of your comfort zone regularly to learn and grow.

Old Habit: Believing that you are either good at something or you are not, and if you fail at something, that means you are not good at it and should quit.

New Habit: Believing that if you are willing to put in the effort, you can always grow and improve and that failing at one thing does not define you as a failure.

What will you do with this new information? I'd love for you to take out a journal and write down some notes and commitments.

Follow me on social media and check our website for more ideas and resources to shift your mindset. I'd also love for you to share your mindset shift experiences in our Facebook Group. You can find both at ownyourcareerownyourlife.com.

CHAPTER FOURTEEN

YOU MUST PRIORITIZE ACTIVITIES TO ACHIEVE YOUR GOALS

If you are going to achieve big goals, you must prioritize the most important things to work on. The mistake many people and companies make is that they either don't take time to prioritize, or they call everything a priority without defining their ranking of importance. If everything is a priority, nothing is a priority, and nothing gets done.

Earlier, I introduced the Eisenhower Matrix and how we need to know when things are important or urgent (or both) to help us decide where to spend our time. If you want to achieve big things, this is something you have to get good at because you only have a certain amount of time available to get things done, and you probably waste a large percentage of it (sorry).

Time

When you think about it, the only finite resource we have is time, though I know that money can also be hard to come by for many people. I have had plenty of money struggles over the years. But the truth is, money is abundant, and if you develop the right skills, find the right job or come up with the right business idea, you can always make more money. There is actually no limit to the amount of money you can make. As I write this, Jeff Bezos is the richest man in the world, worth over $100 billion, and it continues to go up with no limitations. As I continue to learn and help more people, I continue to make more money too.

Though we all have limited time and knowledge, there is no limit on the amount of money we can make. Even if you are an hourly worker or in a union with a defined hourly pay rate, you can always get a second job, start a side business, or quit your job and find one with higher pay. I'm not saying this is easy, but it's always possible.

The only limited resource we have is time. And it's the same for everyone. Every person on this earth has twenty-four hours a day, seven days a week, and 365.25 days per year to get things done.

When you think about how limited time is, you have to think about whether you are using it wisely because everything you do in life has trade-offs.

Everything Has Trade-Offs

When you say yes to one thing, you are saying no to something else. The classic example is to look at how you spend your week—time spent at work vs. time with family and friends vs. having fun with hobbies, etc.

When you decide to do something like stay late at the office to get a project done, you might be missing happy hour, dinner with your family, or the gym. Conversely, when you decide to hit the gym and then have dinner with your spouse or friend, you might be missing an opportunity to get extra work done or get ahead on the next project.

Everything you do in life is a choice. You are making those choices every single day, whether you are doing it consciously or not. With every action you take, you are choosing how to spend your time. I want to think that spending time reading this book is a wise choice (and I hope it pays off), but by reading this book, you are missing an opportunity to read another book, call a friend, or get more work done. Similarly, when you scroll through social media or watch Netflix, you miss an opportunity to read a book like this one to enhance your life.

That is why I think it is important to think more about how we spend our time. Many people drift along, doing what everyone else is doing, potentially wasting valuable time doing things that may not contribute to their goals.

There is no judgment here. You get to decide how you spend your time, and I decide how I spend mine. We all need to relax from time to time. I want to raise awareness and make sure you understand that you have a limited amount of time on this Earth and how you spend it matters. You probably have time to do everything you want to do if you are completely honest with yourself and others.

Be Honest with Yourself and Others

Once I got into personal development and started reading a lot of books and digging into this idea of taking ownership of my life, I noticed a pervasive problem in our society. And that problem is people lying to themselves and others about how much time they have. As mentioned, we all have the same amount of time, and we all choose to use it differently.

I hear people all the time say things like, "I'd like to work out more, but I don't have enough time," or "I'd like to go back to school, but I don't have enough time," or, insert any other ambitious goal with the excuse that they don't have enough time.

Sometimes, it's true, but most of the time, it is not. Most people are lying to themselves and others when they say they don't have time for something. We all have the same amount of time. How we prioritize that time is up to us. I believe we all have enough time to do anything we want if we prioritize effectively. The problem is people waste a lot of time on things without thinking about the trade-offs or considering that they get to decide how they spend their time.

An example is a person that says they don't have time to go to the gym, but they watch two hours of TV each night. I am not judging anyone. Everyone gets to live their life however they want. But if everyone stopped saying, "I don't have time," and started saying, "I chose not to make the time," I think it would cause a significant shift in our society, because we'd stop making so many excuses.

How many times have you told someone you couldn't help them do something or show up to their event because you "didn't have time," when the truth was, you just didn't want to, or it wasn't a priority?

Let's be honest about how much time we have and what we can accomplish. As I mentioned before, everything we do comes down to priorities and trade-offs. If you really wanted to get in shape, you'd work less or watch TV less and hit the gym each day. That's just the truth.

Getting More Done

If you want to get more done and achieve your goals, you've got to get serious about time management and start being honest about what you have time to do and how you are choosing to live your life.

I run a business, host two podcasts, exercise five to seven days a week, am writing a book, planning events, posting almost daily on social media, and I show up daily for my family. People often ask me how I get so much done. The truth is, I have gotten better at prioritization and time management. I've also eliminated a lot of time-wasting activities (like watching sports). And yet, I still feel like I could be more efficient with my time!

You don't have to be like me. It's okay to relax and watch Netflix or football. We all need it. But if you have goals you are working toward, I want you to be honest with yourself and know how you're spending your time so you can prioritize the things that will help you own your life and achieve your goals.

By the way, I don't think there is ever a right or wrong way to spend your time. But when you choose to make time for something (work, family, fitness, play, sports, Netflix, etc.), you have to remember that there is a tradeoff and you will be spending less time on the other things.

So, if you want to get more done, the key is to know your priorities and get serious about how you are spending your time. Then, if you want to see if you are spending your time in the right places, look at your schedule and see if it matches up with your goals.

For example, you might say that family is the most important thing to you (most people do), but if you work eighty hours a week and then play golf with your friends on the weekend, you are either lying or delusional. Conversely, if your goal is to get a promotion or make more money, that may require you to put in some long hours at the office.

Again, everyone's situation is different. If you want to watch sports or play video games, great! Just be honest about how you prioritize your time.

Your Turn

Okay, let's do an exercise. Grab a journal, reference your vision and goals that we set earlier or write them down now. What is your vision, and what are your top goals? Can you put them in order of priority? Do you have a plan for how to get there?

For example, your vision is to be VP of Finance or even CEO one day, and you know you'll need a better network, more recognition, and a few promotions along the way. You might make a plan to work more and prioritize the activities that will get you there. Those might include time for learning, networking, and extra projects to build your reputation. If you have a family, education, or fitness goals, you need to account for those and have an honest conversation with yourself and your family about your goals and how you'll spend your time.

My vision is to be on bigger stages (literal and metaphorical) so that I can influence millions of people to live their lives more intentionally while also showing up for my family – being a great husband and father – and living a great life. That's a big vision, and I know it won't just happen without a lot of effort. So, I have goals and a plan, and I prioritize my time to get as much done as I can each day before having dinner with my family.

What about you? What is your big vision and some of your goals? Does your schedule match? How can you adjust your schedule to help you achieve your goals? Maybe you need to work more or less. Maybe you need to build in more time for networking or building your brand. Maybe you want to get into better shape and need to schedule a time for the gym. And maybe I just made you realize how much time you waste watching sports or the news. (Sorry!).

Whatever it is, write it down, commit to it, tell a friend, and share it in our Facebook Group. Let's talk about habits.

Old Habit: Drifting along, lying to yourself (and others), making excuses, letting others control your time. Procrastinating on the things you know you need or want to do.

New Habit: Taking ownership and responsibility, being honest about how much time you have and how you choose to use it, scheduling time to do the most important things and spending less time on passive, unimportant activities.

New Commitment: Never lie and say, "I didn't have time," when the truth is, you didn't prioritize the activity (which is okay). Instead, say, "I didn't make time."

I would love for you to share your changes in our group and on social media. Use the hashtags #ownyourcareer and #ownyourtime.

CHAPTER SUMMARY

In this chapter, we discussed the importance of prioritizing our time. Most people don't think much about their schedule and how well it aligns with their vision, purpose, and values. They let others drop meetings in and spend hours on passive activities that don't add value (like watching the news, sports, or Netflix). There is nothing wrong with engaging in some of those things, but I want you to be honest about how you are spending your time.

Most people make excuses and lie to themselves and others about what they have time for ("Sorry, I didn't have time to get that done"), and I want you to be more honest so that you can do a better job of prioritizing your time.

By prioritizing the most critical activities, scheduling them each day or week, and being aware of how we are spending our time, we can get a lot more done.

You can find time to do anything you want as long as you make it a priority. What will you prioritize, and how will you change your schedule to get the most important things done? Be sure to let me and others know!

CHAPTER FIFTEEN

HOW TO ACHIEVE BIG GOALS

So far, we've discussed how to own your career and prepare for the future. We've talked about setting big goals several times, and in Chapter 3, we talked about the importance of setting SMART goals.

We've also discussed the importance of having the right mindset, and prioritizing your time. So now that you are ready to stop drifting, own your life, and achieve your big goals, we need to make sure you have a plan and the tools to execute.

The first step is to get clarity on your goals and how they align with your vision. There is no point in setting irrelevant goals (although people do it all the time). We want to set audacious goals that align with your vision and purpose and then commit to doing everything you can to achieve those goals.

Let's talk about some of the things you can do to improve your chances of achieving your goals.

SMART Goals Refresher

First, a quick review. A goal without a plan is just a wish. You need to set SMART goals (Specific, Measurable, Achievable, Relevant, and Time-bound). Your long-term vision might be to one day be CFO or VP of IT. To improve your chances of achieving that vision, you've got to set some SMART goals. For example:

1. I will earn an advanced financial degree or certificate by October by studying three nights per week for the next four months

2. I will get a promotion to XYZ position in the next twelve months by exceeding all expectations in my role and solving new problems in my department

When you make your goals specific and measurable, it becomes easier to track your progress to completion. As they say, "What gets measured, gets done."

Write Them Down

Second, you can increase your chances of achieving your goals by writing them down. According to some studies, you are forty-two percent more likely to achieve your goals when you write them down. Why? Many people say it has to do with the inner workings of our brain and that writing things down activates both the imaginative and logical parts of our brains.

I write my big goals down in a notebook and a whiteboard in my office, so I that can see them regularly. I also keep a document with all of the goals I create every January and then update it throughout the year as necessary. Some gurus (like Grant Cardone) suggest writing your goals daily to remind you of what you are chasing. I don't write them down every day (although I see the benefits), but I do recite them every morning in my morning affirmations, which leads me to my third step.

Establish a Habit to Help You Achieve Your Goal

One of the best things you can do to achieve a big goal is to establish a daily or weekly habit. Most big goals seem daunting until you break them down into daily or weekly activities. Many people set annual or quarterly goals and break them down into monthly, weekly, and daily habits.

For example, if your goal is to take an online course, you need to establish a habit of studying X days per week for Y hours per day. Get as specific as possible (e.g., I will study every Monday, Wednesday, and Thursday 5-7 p.m.). When I was studying for the GMAT to get into business school, I wanted to achieve an excellent score, so I scheduled time to study every weekday afternoon after work for two hours, and it paid off.

If your goal is to get a promotion at work, it's important to know what it will take (talk to your manager to find out), make a plan, and then set weekly habits that will help you get there. Those might include learning, networking, working on special projects, shoring up blind spots, and double-checking the work you turn in. Then, you have something you can track and stick to.

When I decided to write this book, it felt like a huge goal. Instead of worrying about a giant book, I started with an outline and a simple goal and then created a daily habit to get there. My big target was to write 50,000 words, and the daily habit I wanted to establish was to write 500 words per day, seven days a week. I ended up sticking with that habit and finished the first draft of this book in a little over three months. I missed a handful of days but had others where I wrote more than 500 words. Overall, I averaged about 570 words per day, which exceeded my goal, and if you're reading this book, that means I achieved my goal of writing and publishing a book!

Recite Affirmations Daily

Another thing you can do to help you achieve big goals is to either write or recite them daily (or both) as part of affirmations.

I started using affirmations after I read *The Miracle Morning* and have been using them daily ever since. I highly recommend them to help you achieve big goals. An affirmation is simply a reminder of something positive that is true or that you want to be true and can also be part of a goal. For example, every morning, I remind myself that I am worthy and deserving of all the success that comes my way and that I cannot wait or let fears get in my way of achieving big goals. I also recite all of my big goals (usually four to six of them) across different buckets that include family, health, business, financial, etc.

There is a lot of information out there about affirmations (*The Miracle Morning* is a great place to start), so I won't go into it here. But using positive affirmations can go a long way in supporting your mindset as you pursue big goals. Repeating your goals daily can help remind you what you are trying to achieve.

If you want to get a copy of my daily affirmations and the goals I recite each morning, you can find them in the bonus section of our website at ownyourcareerownyourlife.com/bonus.

I got started using affirmations after downloading Hal's from his website years ago, and it would be my honor to help you get started with yours.

Use Social Pressure and Accountability

After writing your goals down and reminding yourself daily (whether you rewrite them or use affirmations or both), the next best thing you can do is to tell a friend or many friends (or your whole network). Why? A few reasons.

First, it's always great to have support. When you tell your friend you are working on getting in shape, they might ask what help you need or check with you from time to time. Or they might even say they want to join you.

Having moral support to root you on is underrated when facing challenging goals. There is a reason why many sports teams perform better in front of a home crowd. They get a boost from the moral support.

Next, telling people about your goals and what you are attempting to do provides social pressure, thus accountability helping to ensure you'll follow through. It's one thing to tell yourself that you will start studying three days a week or that you are going to take on an extra project at work. But if you don't tell anyone, there is no accountability or consequences (nobody will know) if you quit or never even start.

When you tell your friend, manager, or mentor that you are going after a big goal and ask them for accountability, they can check in with you regularly. You'll feel more pressure to keep going because then, quitting means not only giving up on your goals but also potential shame in front of others.

If you want to take your accountability to the next level, you can also share your goals on social media and ask who wants to join you. If you decide to accept some of the challenges in this book and shift your mindset, stop complaining, set a vision, or any of the other steps toward owning your career and life, you can post those goals on social media to declare your commitment and ask who else wants to join you.

I've done this many times and have seen others do it, and it can be quite effective. It not only creates accountability; it often inspires others to jump on board and take action as well. That's the power of community.

If you are ready to take this step, be sure to share in a way that allows others to support you, hold you accountable, and join you if they want. And be sure to use hashtag #ownyourcareerownyourlife.

WARNING: I've read and heard that one potential risk of posting about a goal on social media is that it might trigger something in the brain that makes you feel like you've already accomplished it. I've heard of people posting publicly that they have decided to write a book and receive the congratulations from their network. Then they never write the book because they already feel a sense of accomplishment.

If you post publicly about a goal, the point or purpose of doing so is to give you added accountability to go after it. You are basically asking who wants to join you and hold you accountable. You're not looking for congratulations.

When I started writing this book, I posted a couple of times that I was writing and about my daily goal of writing at least 500 words per day. Then I shared my progress to show I was taking action, hopefully inspiring others to do the same.

If you post publicly about a big goal, try sharing the habit that will help you get there. For example, I will write 500 words per day, go to the gym four times a week, have one coffee networking meeting a week, etc. Then people can check in with you.

Hire a Coach or Join a Mastermind Group

Finally, one of the most effective things you can do to ensure that you achieve your goals is to hire a coach, join a mastermind group, or both.

If you have never hired a coach before, you might want to consider it. You can think of them like a sports coach— someone who helps guide you, motivate you, and push you to achieve your goals. It may seem like a strange concept to some, but the most successful, high performing people all have coaches. Obviously, athletes have coaches. As I write this, Tom Brady is probably the most successful American football quarterback of all time, and he has three coaches (or maybe more) to constantly help him improve.

If you work in a company, perhaps you've been provided an executive coach, or noticed that the top executives all have coaches. That is key to helping them develop strengths and improve on weaknesses

If you want to change careers, you may want to consider hiring a life, career, or performance coach. I have personally worked with a few coaches and always find it beneficial. And any time I set a big goal, I make sure I have a coach, mentor, or mastermind group to support me. I never assume I can figure things out on my own. That's too frustrating.

For example, when I decided to write this book, I didn't want to try and figure things out on my own, so, I invested in a course and coaching program run by my friend, Honorée Corder. Honorée has published more than fifty books and knows all the ins and outs of the process. This book is a big deal for me, and I want it to be successful, so I invested in a course to learn from the best person I could find, and that was Honorée.

I also mentioned mastermind groups. A mastermind group comprises like-minded, ambitious professionals who meet regularly to challenge and support each other in their goals. The phrase was coined by Napoleon Hill in *Think And Grow Rich*, referring to how industry titans like Henry Ford and Dale Carnegie met regularly to support each other.

I read that book and joined my first mastermind group in 2016 and have been in mastermind groups consistently ever since. I love the coaching I get from the people who run them and the camaraderie and support I get from the other members. As I write this, I'm in two different mastermind groups for entrepreneurs and love it.

Over the years, I have invested thousands of dollars in personal development programs, coaching, and mastermind groups, and it has always paid off.

I will likely start a mastermind group for ambitious career professionals after publishing this book, so check our website or Facebook Group to find more information.

Track Your Progress and Use Streaks

Finally, you've got to find a way to track your progress so that you can see how you're doing to make adjustments along the way. They say, "What gets measured, gets done," which means that when there is a way to measure progress, it's a lot more likely you'll achieve the goal. Just think about status reports at work and how you scramble to get things done when you know your boss is checking in. It's the same with your goals.

I keep a daily journal where I can write down daily and weekly goals and check on progress. I also use spreadsheets and a Customer Relationship Management (CRM) tool to track all my client outreach.

Jerry Seinfeld, the famous comedian, is known for setting a goal to write at least one joke every single day and then crossing the days off the calendar when he did. He said his goal was to do it daily and never "break the chain" of joke writing. By doing that, he established a habit, got more practice, and thus regularly created content.

If your goal is to learn new skills to help with a career change, perhaps you can set a goal to learn or practice for at least ten minutes every single day and track that with a journal, spreadsheet, or calendar.

If your goal is to build a bigger network, you could set a goal to connect with at least one new person or have one conversation every weekday, and then create a spreadsheet or calendar to tick the days off and see how long you can keep the streak going.

Your Turn

Now it's time to establish those goals and figure out how you are going to track them. Don't leave this chapter without writing some things down. Take out that journal, declare your goals, and how you will track progress.

What goals will you pursue? What habits will you establish? Who will support you and hold you accountable? Whom do you need help from? How can you track and measure progress?

Changing Habits

As we discussed previously, to be successful, we need to establish new habits. What habits will you establish to achieve your goals?

Old Habit: Not setting big goals, not writing them down, or sharing with others. Holding back for fear of failure.

New Habit: Setting big goals, making them SMART, writing them down and sharing them with others with the knowledge that this habit will help you achieve more.

CHAPTER SUMMARY

There is a ton of information available on how to achieve goals. I have used much of it to attempt big goals. I even achieved a lot of them, but not all. Sometimes when you set a big goal, you don't achieve it, but you grow into someone who takes regular action to go after it.

To achieve the vision you wrote down earlier, you've got to be willing to set big goals and make them SMART. That means they are Specific, Measurable, Achievable, Relevant, and Time-bound. Remember that "What gets measured, gets done."

If you want to increase your chances of achieving your goals:

1. Write them down.

2. Establish daily or weekly habits to make progress.

3. Revisit them daily via affirmations or writing them daily.

4. Find an accountability partner or group.

5. Post on social media for extra accountability.

6. Hire a coach or join a mastermind group.

If you need more help, check out our website for resources, and don't forget to share your goals and new habits on social media, tag me, and use the hashtags #ownyourlife #accountability.

CHAPTER SIXTEEN

DEALING WITH COMPARISON

Since I got into personal development and started my podcasts, I've spent a lot of time interviewing and studying successful people, what drives them, and what holds them back. I've also spent a lot of time analyzing my own strengths, weaknesses, and the psychology of what brings me down or holds me back.

One of the most common factors that holds people back is comparison. More specifically, comparing ourselves to everyone around us—what we think about ourselves in light of what we think about others because we never know the real story.

That has been a problem plaguing people for decades, if not longer. You see that your coworker has a nicer car, house, or better marriage than you, or their kids seem better behaved. You start comparing and ask yourself why you don't have it as good as them. All we need to do is look at the people around us (at home, work, school, church), and we instantly start comparing to see if we measure up.

Part of this is natural. It's how we benchmark our lives to see if we are doing the right things, or at least to know what others are doing. It has been going on for generations.

But what has changed drastically over the last twenty years is social media, especially the ability to see pictures and videos of people showing the highlights of their lives daily on Instagram and Facebook.

Have you ever looked at someone's post and thought their life or job is better than yours, or they have it all figured out, and you don't? If so, you're not alone. It's also not true. What people share on social media and show off in life is usually more of their highlight reel—the best parts of their lives, not the challenges or mistakes they've made. You have to remember that no matter what you see publicly, you don't know what's going on behind the scenes—inside their head, inside their house, inside their marriage or, inside their career.

Everyone has problems, challenges, strengths, and weaknesses. And everyone is on their own journey. Yes, we should all be striving to improve, and there is much we can learn from others. But nobody has it completely figured out. Nobody's life is perfect. If you find people with seemingly perfect lives, you can either learn from them, be inspired by them, or ignore them. But it never helps to compare yourself to them.

The Mindset Shift to Overcome Comparison

I have made many shifts to overcome this challenge, and I want to share some tips that have helped me, though I am far from perfect and still struggle with comparing myself to those around me. Some of that is good, and some holds me back. I'm on this journey of growth and improvement, just like you. Here are some of the lessons that have helped me:

1. Success is not a zero-sum game, and there is an abundance of success available

2. Shift from a mindset of scarcity to one of abundance - We are not really in competition with anyone else

3. Everyone has challenges – nobody has it all figured out

4. Instead of comparing yourself to those you consider successful, try being inspired by them, and ask what you can learn from them

5. Use someone else's success as motivation for you to achieve big things as well

Let's break some of these down.

From Scarcity to Abundance

First of all, know that success is not a zero-sum game. There are no limits on success (or money for that matter). If you want to make more money, get in better shape, or have a happier marriage, you have the power to create it. Nobody's success is preventing you. Sure, I can see a situation where your department at work has only one director or VP position available, and it might get taken by someone already in that role or someone who outperforms you. But that does not limit your ability to get another job, change roles, make more money, or decide to be happy in the job you have. There is no limit on success and happiness. Remembering this one fact can help you shift your mindset from one of scarcity to one of abundance.

Second, when you shift your mindset from one of scarcity to one of abundance, not only will you be able to attract more success, but you'll be more likable and probably more fulfilled. I have personally made this shift, and it feels great to root for others knowing their success does not prevent me from achieving mine.

If you haven't heard these terms before, having a scarcity mindset means you believe there is a limited amount of something, and you need to protect it. Examples include being frugal with money or protective of clients because you are afraid you won't get more. The most toxic example I see in the corporate world is employees sabotaging each other, or worse, a manager holding an employee back because they are afraid the employee might take their job. It's a shame these things happen because that means the manager is living in fear and will probably never be truly happy.

When you shift to a mindset of abundance, you believe there is plenty of success, money, clients, jobs, promotions, etc. available for everyone, and you don't need to hoard what you have or root against others.

It is true that this mindset might make you more vulnerable to someone stealing your job, promotion, client, etc., but I think the risk is well worth it.

Choose to Be Inspired

If you are ambitious and competitive like I am, it's common to feel envious when you see others succeed. It has happened to me many times. I'm building a business and personal brand as well as hosting podcasts and writing a book, and I know dozens of other great people doing similar things, so it is hard not to compare myself.

One important thing I have tried to do is choose to be inspired instead of discouraged when others achieve success. Because, as I mentioned earlier, there is no shortage of success. If someone I know gains a ton of followers, writes a best-selling book, or makes a ton of money, I try to appreciate what they've done and say something like, "Wow! That is cool. If they can do that, then so can I. There is no reason I can't." You can do the same when your friend or colleague achieves a promotion before you or seems to love their job more.

In addition to them showing us what's possible, we can also ask what we can learn from them. Have they been building the foundation for a long time? Do they manage their time better, have mentors, or different skills? We can learn something from everyone who has achieved the things we want to emulate.

So next time you see someone get a promotion or achieve something you also want to achieve, instead of getting lost in envy, try asking what you can learn from their success. Then use their success as inspiration to achieve your own success.

And finally, remember that we are all on a journey. You may not realize half of what others went through to get where they are today—you don't know what else is going on in their life. Maybe they are crushing it at work, but their marriage is on the rocks, or they are out of shape because they spend all their time at the office and no time at the gym. And they just might be jealous or envious of you for some reason as well.

Remember, there are trade-offs to everything, and nobody's life is perfect. Everyone has challenges. You shouldn't compare your whole life to someone else's highlight reel.

Instead, look at what they've accomplished and either ask, "How can I be inspired by them and learn from them?" or move on.

Bonus: If you want to take this mindset shift to the next level, I would suggest connecting with several people who have achieved the success you want and ask them to share some of their journey and advice. You can also offer help to those who want to achieve what you have. People love helping others, and everyone wins when we do this.

Self-Awareness

I've already talked a few times about the importance of self-awareness. But I want to mention it again because the more you get to know (and love) yourself, the more comfortable you become with who you are, where you are on your journey, and where you want to go. That allows you to avoid getting held back by imposter syndrome and comparison. When you genuinely know and love yourself, know where you want to go, and enjoy the journey, you can be happy and not worry about keeping up with others.

We are all individuals with different personalities, strengths, weaknesses, and circumstances. Life is not a competition. So, let's just be ourselves, love who we are, and try to get better together.

For more great advice on how to deal with comparison, check out the book *Measuring Up: How to WIN in a World of Comparison* by my friend Renee Vidor. In her book, she explains what causes us to get caught up in comparison and gives some great advice for dealing with it.

CHAPTER SUMMARY

One of the biggest things that holds high achievers back is comparison.

It's been a problem for decades and has been exacerbated by social media and the ability to see everyone's highlights all the time. I have struggled with this as well.

To beat this, we have to shift our mindset from scarcity to abundance. We have to realize that success is not limited and that we get to create our own success. Therefore, there is no reason to be competitive, overprotective, root against others, or be discouraged when others succeed. Instead, with a mindset of abundance, we can root for others, knowing that their success does not limit ours. And we can choose to be inspired by them.

If someone achieves something we also want (money, promotion, etc.), we can choose to be inspired by them and ask what we can learn from them. Maybe they will even become a mentor or coach for us.

All this requires is a mindset shift and new habits that will create more happiness, fulfillment, and success.

Old Habit: Being competitive, believing there is a limited amount of success, rooting against others, and getting discouraged when others achieve success. Having a mindset of scarcity.

New Habit: Being collaborative, believing there is an unlimited amount of success, rooting for everyone around you to succeed because if they succeed, so can you. Having a mindset of abundance. Believing in your abilities to succeed and that you deserve the success that comes your way.

Take a moment to write down what mindset shifts you need to make to achieve more success.

CHAPTER SEVENTEEN

ADDITIONAL STRATEGIES TO HELP YOU OWN YOUR CAREER AND LIFE

Over the years, I have put into practice many strategies that have helped me achieve big goals and take more ownership of my life. I have so much to share but limited space to share it. When I wrote all of this down, my wife told me it was too long and needed to be a separate book in itself. So, for now, I will give you a few snippets, and I will plan to share more in the bonus materials on my website and write more in my next book (stay tuned!).

With that said, here are some additional strategies you can use to help you own your career and life and take control of your future.

1. Having a morning routine
2. Taking care of your health: sleep, meditation, nutrition, fitness
3. Using a journal
4. Regular reading and learning and regular introspection
5. Finding mentors, coaches, mastermind groups
6. Helping others
7. Having a bias for action (progress > perfection)

As I mentioned, this chapter probably could be a book in itself, so I'm going to give a short bit about each one and share more later as the demand arises.

You don't have to do all of these every day or week, but it would be valuable to review them and think about whether you would like to start doing them. Perhaps some of them you are already doing and some you've never done before.

The Importance of a Morning Routine

I have already talked about how reading *The Miracle Morning* changed my life. Hal's book introduced me to the power of having a strong, intentional, and productive morning routine

The whole idea behind a morning routine (and the reason it's so powerful) is that you start your day about an hour before you need to, and use that time for intentional activities to help you achieve your goals. This way, you start the day by accomplishing some very important things before getting into reactive mode. So, instead of getting up at 8 a.m. to get ready to start work by 9 a.m., you get up at 7 a.m. to do important things like meditate, read, write, check goals, or exercise.

My Morning Routine

My morning routine is based on the morning routine that Hal lays out in *The Miracle Morning*. That includes meditation, affirmations, visualization, exercise, reading, and writing in a journal.

On a typical weekday, I get up at 4:30 or 5 am (I know, pretty early). The first thing I do is drink some water (very important), and then I start the coffee. While it's brewing, I sit and meditate for ten minutes. Then I grab my first cup of coffee and head out for a walk around the block while I recite my affirmations and think about my day.

Once I return, I open a book and start reading for fifteen to twenty minutes with my journal nearby in case I need to make notes. Then, when I come to a good stopping place in the book, I open up my journal to write down my gratitude (a really important practice) and plan my day. I also worked on this book every morning for several months as part of my routine. And finally, I will head to the gym for a workout or get started on some important work if I decide to go to the gym later.

You Do You

I shared my morning routine, which is based on what Hal Elrod teaches in his book, *The Miracle Morning*. You can modify it or do whatever you choose whenever you like. If you are a night owl and hate mornings, do this stuff at night instead of watching Netflix. The most important thing is that you dedicate time in your day to be intentional about your health and personal development and not drifting or reacting to others.

In Chapter 8, I mentioned the importance of sharpening the saw. Unfortunately, very few people invest time consistently to learn, grow, and improve their health. You don't have to be most people. Make sure you block time daily for these activities.

Old Habit: Getting up at the last minute, starting the day in reaction mode, and making little time for intentional habits like meditation, reading, and writing.

New Habit: Waking up earlier than necessary and making time for important habits like meditation, affirmations, reading, writing, and exercise.

Take Care of Your Health

It's astounding to me how many people choose to ignore this critical component of their lives. They say things like, "I'm too busy to get to the gym," or "I work too much. I don't have time to eat healthy." Really?

I know life and work can be demanding. I know there is a lot of pressure out there to perform. Many people have long commutes, demanding bosses, limited financial resources, and other priorities (spouses, kids, volunteering, hobbies, etc.). And I know that everyone's situation is different. But if you don't take care of your health, there could be major consequences that render everything else irrelevant.

Investing in your health has both short-term and long-term benefits. In the short-term, you get more energy, productivity, and happiness. In the long-term, you get to live a longer, healthier life and spend less on healthcare.

Yes, I know every situation is different, and even the healthiest person can get hit by a bus or get cancer at forty. I've seen it. But on average, those who choose to invest in their health will live longer, healthier, happier lives and become positive role models for their family and friends.

The key components of this are sleep, diet, and exercise. I would add meditation and mindfulness for mental health as well.

Getting Sleep

The importance of sleep is not talked about enough. Most people don't get enough. I probably don't get enough. The Centers for Disease Control (CDC) says that at least one in three Americans don't get enough sleep.

So, what is enough sleep? That depends on the person. Some people need eight hours per night, and some are fine on six to eight, but most people should get at least six.

My goal is always eight hours, but I'm usually in the six to eight-hour range and seem to operate well on that. I also do things to enhance my sleep, like getting to bed before 10 p.m., leaving my iPhone in another room, making the bedroom as dark as possible, and turning the thermostat down at night. For information about why I do these things (and why you should too), I recommend you read the book Sleep Smarter: 21 Essential Strategies to *Sleep Your Way to A Better Body, Better Health, and Bigger Success* by Shawn Stevenson. There are some great studies and suggestions in that book that have helped a lot of people.

Eating Healthy

I don't think I need to say much about the importance of nutrition and eating a healthy diet. There is a ton of information available, and yet most people are eating like crap. Even I fall off the wagon a bit sometimes. But we have to remember that not only is eating healthy a long-term investment in our longevity, but eating healthy, nutritious foods can give us more energy, strength, and even creativity and intelligence during the workweek.

When you think about things like that, choosing a salad over a burger could help you with the next big idea that makes you more money.

Here's what my diet looks like in a typical week. I eat eggs, bacon, and some bread in the morning with my kids. I usually make a giant smoothie (with tons of fruit) for lunch, and then have a dinner of protein and vegetables with my family. We generally keep a lot of produce in the house and try to eat mostly whole, real foods, and avoid processed foods (but we do have a few things like pretzels, Clif Bars, etc.).

A very simple rule for eating healthy is to prepare most of your food at home and stay on the outside aisles of the grocery store (bread, meat, produce), and avoid the middle aisles (all processed foods). I don't think it needs to be much more complicated than that.

Importance of Activity and Exercise

If you choose one thing to stay healthy and fit, I think diet and nutrition are the most important. The next is simply moving and getting some level of exercise. While more and more intense is better, even taking a few walks throughout the day and shooting for at least 10,000 steps can go a long way to improving your health.

I strive to take a few walks and also get a workout at least once a day.

Sometimes that means we need to get creative, especially if a global pandemic closes your gym (like it did mine). During that time, I took my kids to the park for exercise and did a lot of pushups at home. I know many other people have home gyms or find time to take walks, runs, or bike rides when they can.

If you are unsure of what kind of exercise you should do, I recommend reading some books or hiring a trainer to get you started. I believe strongly in the benefits of resistance training (lifting weights) for everyone, so I typically lift weights three or four days a week and play basketball or get cardio in a couple times a week. I also do yoga and ride my bike on the weekends. I am a big fan of yoga for mental and physical health, so if you haven't tried it, give it a shot.

For more information on the benefits of lifting and what types of exercises to do, I recommend the book *Bigger Leaner Stronger: The Simple Science of Building the Ultimate Male Body* by Michael Matthews. That book is easy to follow, backed by science, and changed how I worked out a few years ago, with excellent results.

And of course, there are tons of other books, podcasts, and resources out there to help you get healthy and fit. I will put a list of books, blogs, and podcasts in our website's bonus resources section so you can get the info you need. If you have suggestions that I should add, let me know. Just go to ownyourcareerownyourlife.com/bonus to get access.

Finally, don't be afraid to ask for help. We all need help in certain areas, and there is no point in assuming you should be able to figure it out on your own. I have been working out regularly for twenty plus years, and I still read and follow experts to improve.

> **Old Habit:** Spending your life in reaction mode, putting work above health and sleep.
>
> **New Habit:** Being intentional about what you eat, how often you exercise, how much sleep you get, and making health a priority.

Use a Journal

I have been using a daily journal for a few years now and have found many benefits. Some people like to use journals to record musings and thoughts, some to record the things happening in their life, and many (like me) use a journal to keep them on track with goals.

While I do record thoughts, ideas, and moments from my life in my journals, the primary reasons I use a journal are to check with my schedule every morning, write down the most important things I need to get done, and then reflect on the day before I go to sleep at night. I also like to use the journal to write down my gratitude every morning (note: I highly recommend a regular gratitude practice to decrease stress and increase happiness).

When I first started, I bought a blank journal and wrote freely each day. Later I got more structured journals with regular entries. What you use is up to you, but I do recommend using something. As I mentioned previously, writing down and tracking your goals is a great way to improve your chances of success. And having a journal allows you to write, record, and review goals daily.

I am creating a companion journal for this book called the *Own Your Career Own Your Life* Companion Journal (check our website or Amazon for info) and there are many other great journals out there. One I've used a lot over the last few years is *The Freedom Journal* by John Lee Dumas, which helps you track progress of a 100 day goal. I've also used *The 5-minute Journal* and *Full Focus Planner* by Michael Hyatt and gotten value from them.

There are tons of great journals out there that you can try and they all have different pros and cons, but they all work. Pick one, start, and then try new journals as you go. Do what works for you.

Old Habit: Drifting along in reaction mode without planning or recording any thoughts or progress toward goals.

New Habit: Using a daily journal to record thoughts, ideas, gratitude, important tasks, and progress toward goals.

Regular Reading, Learning, and Introspection

Earlier in this book, I talked about the importance of continuous learning and sharpening the saw to keep growing and improving, so I don't want to beat a dead horse. If you're

s book, I already know you are interested in learn-
)wing.

)mpelled to remind you that the world is changing
fast, and if you are not growing, you might be doing the opposite (shrinking or dying). You pick. I feel like I need growth
to be happy and fulfilled, which is why I make time to learn
regularly.

As I already said, nobody has it all figured out, and the
most successful people I know (especially those with a strong
growth mindset) are constantly reading, learning, and finding
ways to grow.

One of the most important ways you can do that is to
make time to read each day (whether you like physical books,
e-books, or audiobooks doesn't matter) and listen to podcasts. You can also do other things to learn and develop.

Along with that, I suggest you give yourself space and permission regularly for introspection. What that means is that
you spend time reflecting on the things you learn from others
(and yourself) and look for ways to improve. Examine your
strengths and weaknesses, examine your thoughts and actions, and look for ways to improve. We can always improve.

That is where the morning routine comes in handy. I have
space every morning to read and write. I usually spend some
time in thought as well. I like to check in with myself now
and again when I'm having thoughts or reacting to things a
certain way.

So, if you are not already doing it, make sure you start
scheduling a regular time to make that happen. I firmly believe that most fulfillment comes from growth.

And if you are already reading and learning regularly (like
this book), I recommend you take time for introspection after

you read new things to see how you can put them into practice to improve your life.

I did not write this book simply to open your eyes and give you things to think about. I want you to change your behaviors, take some action, and take full ownership of your career and life. That's why I include these habit change sections.

Old Habit: Spending your life in reaction mode, not making time to read or learn, and when you do, quickly moving onto the next thing without reflecting (I'm guilty of this as well).

New Habits: Make regular time to read and learn from books, podcasts, courses, etc. and spend time reflecting on your life, strengths, weaknesses, personality, and how you can use the tools you are learning to constantly improve.

Find Mentors, Coaches, and Mastermind Groups

Earlier, I discussed getting help and the benefits of having mentors, coaches, and support groups. Humans are social creatures, not built to do things on our own. Some people do, but most of the time, when you hear that someone is "self-made," the truth is, they likely had plenty of help along the way. And if they didn't, they are an anomaly.

I have greatly benefited from the support I've gained from friends, mentors, coaches, and the mastermind groups I've been a part of for the last few years.

So how can you find these resources?

A **mentor** is someone who has achieved the type of things you would like to achieve and is, therefore, qualified to give you advice on your journey. They could be a senior executive or someone one to two levels ahead of you at work. They could also be someone who has started a successful business, achieved financial success, lost weight, or achieved some other goal that you also want to achieve.

The best way to find a mentor is through networking. The best way to appeal to a mentor (and get them excited to work with you) is by finding ways to give them value.

Ideally, you form a relationship with a mentor and can help each other. Maybe you are knowledgeable about something he or she doesn't know how to do, or maybe you can help out with a project or some other task. Maybe their kid needs tutoring in math. Everybody needs help with something.

When you approach a potential mentor, ask questions. Get to know them and see if you can help in any way. Ask if they would be willing to share some of their experience and advice with you. You might ask them to formally mentor you, but I know that puts some people off because of the pressure or assumed time commitment; so often, it could be better to just let things happen naturally.

A **coach** can ask you powerful questions and help you figure out where you want to go with your career, business, or life. It can be helpful for that person to be ahead of you on your journey, but that's not required. They don't even need to be better or more talented than you in whatever you do. Think of athletes or musicians who have coaches not nearly as talented as them, but who can see the overall strategy and give advice on how to practice and execute more effectively.

I have discovered I can be a good coach because I like to ask questions and challenge people, which is what coaches do. They don't have to be more skilled.

Coaches are usually paid, and often in the corporate world, you see companies providing executive coaches for senior leaders. If you are not there yet and want a coach, you may have to find one and pay for them yourself. Depending on your goals and budget, this could be a great investment. I think more people should do it. But if money is tight, consider asking a supportive friend if you can coach each other. There are plenty of books and resources on effective coaching, and one I recommend is *The Coaching Habit* by Michael Bungay Stanier, who has been on my podcast twice and spoke at my first conference.

Finally, I mentioned **mastermind groups**. I have already talked about these and how they have helped me navigate my career over the last few years. To find a great mastermind group, you could do a search, but again (like with mentors and coaches), the best way is networking. I've also noticed that most of the experts and influencers that I follow (especially in coaching and entrepreneurship) run masterminds or group coaching programs and I have joined a few of them.

So, if you follow any authors, speakers, experts, or influencers on social media, go to their website and see what they are up to. They may offer coaching or mastermind groups, which is a quick way to learn from them. You can also come to our free Own Your Career Own Your Life Facebook Group and ask people if they know any good ones. If there is enough interest, I might start one as well.

Helping, Coaching, Mentoring, and Teaching Others

If you've ever looked at the most effective ways people learn, they say that it starts with reading or listening to something, then writing it down, and finally practicing it. And then, the most effective way to reinforce learning is to teach others.

If you are someone like me who gets help from many places, you'll want to give back along the way by helping others. You may not think you are qualified, but remember, we are all in different places on our journey.

I heard a great metaphor once from my friend Larry Hagner, who said it's like we are all climbing a mountain roped together. Some of us are way up ahead in certain areas, and some of us are behind, while some of us are in the middle. And it's different in different areas. So, you may feel like you're at the bottom of the mountain in your career, but maybe you have fitness figured out, have a great marriage, or are good at some hobby. The point is that we all need help in some areas, and we can always help others as well.

It's especially true when it comes to careers. Even if you feel like you are at the bottom rung of the ladder, there are still college or high school kids you could mentor and help them figure out where to go next.

By mentoring or coaching others, not only do you get satisfaction, but you also build your network (you never know where those people will end up), and you will often learn more about yourself as well.

So, even if you feel a bit behind and seek help from others, don't forget to also mentor, coach, teach, and help those behind you, because we are all in this journey together, and everyone needs help from someone.

Old Habit: Thinking you can do everything yourself or that coaches are only for athletes and executives.

New Habit: Realizing that everyone needs help and you are worth investing in yourself by finding a mentor, hiring a coach, or joining a mastermind group.

Having a Bias for Action

We've talked a lot about what success means and how to achieve it. We've talked about creating a vision, setting goals, and getting help. We've talked about the most common things that hold people back. I want you to have a plan for your life and for the next thirty days and specific goals you can track. And I want so badly for you to achieve those goals, which is why I need to tell you this.

One of the biggest things that separate those who achieve big success from those who don't is action.

Many people set a goal or make a plan and then freeze up because the timing isn't right, the plan isn't perfect, or they are afraid of what might happen if they fail (or even if they succeed).

Don't let this be you.

Once you set a big goal and break it down into monthly, weekly, or daily milestones, the next thing you need to do is make a commitment and take some action.

One of the biggest reasons I'm able to achieve so much is that I never wait for things to be perfect. I just start taking action and then adjust along the way. I had the idea to write this book, so I made a plan and started writing.

I am lucky that I have never been a perfectionist (quite the opposite, actually). I'd probably make a bad auditor or accountant. There are some areas, like accounting and surgery, that call for perfection. But for most of the goals we are setting, I prefer you to focus on progress over perfection and having a bias for action.

When you have a bias for action, that means you decide you want to do something, you make a brief plan if necessary, and then you start taking action. You don't get bogged down with waiting for the timing to be "perfect." You just take action.

If you want to get a promotion or change careers, you want to start with a goal and plan, but it won't happen until you start taking action—doing extra work, networking, building your brand, etc. Remember, a bias for action and progress over perfection will serve you well.

So, what action(s) can you take today to move you closer to your goal?

Old Habit: Waiting for things to be perfect before moving forward.

New Habit: Taking incremental actions to make progress without worrying too much about things being perfect or possibly failing the first time. That is how we learn and improve.

CHAPTER SUMMARY

We've covered a lot of ground in this chapter. And as I mentioned before, it could be a whole book (and maybe one day it will be). In this chapter, we reviewed seven of the most important things that I think have led to my success, and that could help you immensely as well.

Those seven things are:

1. Having a morning routine
2. Taking care of your health: sleep, meditation, nutrition, fitness
3. Using a journal
4. Regular reading and learning and regular introspection
5. Finding mentors, coaches, mastermind groups
6. Helping others
7. Having a bias for action (progress > perfection)

Each one of these can help you immensely, and when you put them all together, you will be firing on all cylinders.

When you review the list, which ones are you already doing, which do you need to start, and which do you need to do more of?

Bonus: If any of these concepts are new to you or you are just getting started, I know it can be helpful to have specific examples, which is why I'm putting a resource section together for you that you can access on our website: ownyourcareerownyourlife.com/bonus

You can also ask questions and connect with others on this journey by joining our free Own Your Career, Own Your Life Facebook Group.

And if you are starting any new healthy habits, please be sure to find an accountability partner (or coach), post about it on social media (and in our group), and tag me or add the hashtags #ownyourcareerownyourlife and #ownyourlife.

I love to see people taking action!

CONCLUSION

Congratulations on finishing this book! We have covered a lot of ground.

If you are just starting with this idea of owning your career, owning your life, and owning your future, this may be overwhelming. I've included a ton of information and advice and a lifetime worth of wisdom and knowledge. So, remember that you don't need to do everything at once. Achieving big goals starts with small actions. An old Chinese proverb says, "The journey of a thousand miles begins with a single step."

Now you need to decide what your next step is going to be.

When you set big goals, break them down into smaller goals and habits, and then make a plan to achieve those, just like I did with this book. When I started writing this book on January 1st, my big goal was to publish a book that would probably be around 50,000 words. That seemed huge. So, I broke it down into a daily habit of 500 words per day and stuck with it. As I write these words, I'm passing 60,000 words. Pretty cool, right?

So, let's review what we covered in this book:

Own Your Career

We talked about the importance of setting a vision. You don't have to know exactly where you are going (my career has had many twists and turns), but it's helpful to have a target or an idea of what you want to do or learn.

If you can connect that vision to a great purpose that serves you, that's even better. What drives you? What is your "why" for getting up in the morning and going to work?

Then you need to make a plan and set some SMART goals that you can measure so you can start making progress and keep growing.

Finally, we talked about taking ownership of your goals and actions and getting help where you need it (from your manager, mentor, peers, colleagues, friends, family, etc.). And if you have a manager, it's very important that you have a conversation with them to get aligned and get their support.

Have you done these things? Have you written them down yet? Have you shared them with a friend yet? Have you shared them in our Facebook Group?

Own Your Future

Remember that business, work, jobs, and the world are changing fast. You can't count on things staying the same or your job still being the same (or even existing) in a few years. That's why we must always take actions to own our future and be prepared for whatever comes. They say that fortune favors the bold and that luck is what happens when preparation meets hard work. Those who put in the work to prepare will get "lucky" with the best jobs and future opportunities.

To help you prepare and own your future, you've got to continue to...

Invest in continuous education so that you are always learning new things and keeping up with the latest trends. Don't let your knowledge get stagnant. Keep reading, listening to podcasts, taking courses, following experts on LinkedIn, and learning as much as you can. My mantra is to "stay hungry" and keep learning as much as I can.

Build your network. Most opportunities in life come from relationships, and you never know where the next one will come from. To this end, I highly recommend you spend time consistently building your network. That includes internally at your company and externally via networking events, conferences, and social media. Reach out to people, start conversations, be curious, and seek to help. I promise you will reap the benefits.

Build your personal or professional brand. This is not just for entrepreneurs. Most promotions and business opportunities are not based on performance. Instead, they are based on perceptions, which means your brand. You've got to be intentional (and authentic) in building the brand you want people to see.

Have you done these things? Have you written down goals and made commitments? Have you started a daily or weekly habit of connecting with people and posting content? If not, let's get it done!

Own Your Life

Step one is to stop drifting. Stop doing things just because that's what everyone else is doing. And stop wasting time. We only get one life, and I want to live mine with intention and truly own my life. I know you do as well.

We talked about the importance of mindset and how we determine our happiness. No doubt, there will be challenges along the way, and how we perceive and react to those challenges will determine our happiness, fulfillment, and how we influence others. Having a "growth" mindset is important to achieve significant success.

Remember that if you want to achieve big goals, your mindset is critical. Once you have that right, you need to get specific and set SMART goals. Then write them down, tell a friend, and find an accountability buddy or group (or post on social media) to keep you on track.

Finally, I shared some best practices that have helped me achieve success and that I think can help you as well. These included the morning routine, taking care of our health, using a journal to track progress, regular reading, learning and introspection, having mentors, coaches, and mastermind groups, helping and mentoring others, and having a bias for action.

So, where are you on these things? Did you just read them, nod, and move on? Or did you write some things down that you want to start doing?

I hope you enjoyed this book, but it will be worthless to you and a failure to me if you don't take some action. So, what steps are you taking? I'd love for you to share them with me and the world. If you share on social media, don't forget to tag me and use the hashtag #ownyourcareerownyourlife.

Finally, remember that I am providing a plethora of additional resources on our website ownyourcareerownyourlife. com/bonus.

I wish you the best of luck on your journey, and remember, nobody cares more about your career or life than you do, and we only get one shot. So, let's make it count!

PERSONAL REQUEST

Thank you for reading this book. If it was helpful at all, I would be so grateful if you'd share with friends (and on social) and leave a review on Amazon. Those reviews are like gold to authors like me and help others find the book and decide whether to read it or not.

Don't forget to post and share on social media. It will help you build your personal brand and help me spread the word about this movement to own our lives.

BONUS RESOURCES

Throughout this book, I've made many recommendations, and I know people will need more help. I've also started to collect a lot of input from my network on things like career mistakes, advice, health resources, etc. I will put all of these in the bonus resources on my website so you can get access to everything you need. Just go to ownyourcareerownyourlife. com/bonus to get them.

I will also share some advice and mistakes there.

APPENDIX

Top Advice for Corporate Professionals

Over the last three years, I have interviewed hundreds of professionals and asked many of them for their top piece of career advice to help others accelerate their success. I recently went through all my notes and organized the advice into the top six most common themes.

You may notice there is some overlap between categories, and they are often related. I think that is natural. Doing one thing well leads to doing others well.

So, I recommend you read this a few times, embrace it, choose which advice resonates most with you, and then take action.

And if you need help, don't be afraid to ask for it. We will be having lots of great conversations about this in our Facebook Group and the other communities I run.

So, here is a countdown of the top six most common pieces of advice for corporate professionals:

6. Have a "Growth Mindset"

One of the top books recommended on the podcast (and by me) is *Mindset: The New Psychology of Success* by Dr. Carol

Dweck. In that book, Dr. Dweck talks about the importance of having a growth mindset vs. a fixed mindset (which we discussed in Chapter 13).

Reading Dr. Dweck's book had a huge impact on me and how I approach business and life. Doing so with a growth mindset has served me well. And we have had many guests recommend that you approach your work with a similar mindset.

Some of the advice I heard from my podcast guests on this topic included, "Have a growth mindset and don't be afraid to fail," from my friend Anthony Fryar who runs talent development at AppDirect.

Susan Rusconi from Splunk advised us to "embrace the growth mindset and always be in pilot mode." Jessica Amortegui, who formerly ran talent development at Logitech before moving to LinkedIn, said it is important to "Experiment, create, test, adjust, and keep going."

The gist of this advice is that we need to be willing to take chances, try new things, not be afraid to fail, and make adjustments along the way.

Big results, big changes, big success only favor the bold. Those who take chances get out of their comfort zone and don't let failures define them. And that is what it means to operate with a growth mindset.

Questions:

1. Have you been operating with a growth mindset?

2. Are you trying enough new things and getting out of your comfort zone?

3. Are you experimenting and iterating?

5. Set a Vision and Focus

I took some liberties here and grouped several pieces of advice under one category called "Focus." It's all about finding your area of expertise, going deep on something, focusing on what you want to achieve, and not letting distractions get in your way.

For example, the advice I heard from Bonnie Houston, the Chief HR Officer at National Oilwell Varco (NOV) in Houston, was to "Resist the urge to hop on every trend that you read about."

Meredith Lubitz, who built an award-winning women's leadership program at Dow Jones, recommended we "Start with the end in mind." And "Be clear on the destination and be okay with asking for help."

I have also found that many successful people achieve big things because they are clear on their vision and destination, set big goals, and remain focused on achieving those goals no matter what.

Finally, Sam Haider, former Global Head of Talent at ResMed in San Diego, said it is important to "Make development plans multi-year and execute wherever it takes you." In other words, look forward three to five years, set a vision, set big goals, and start executing. And then (leveraging that growth mindset from #6), don't be afraid to pivot.

Questions:

1. Do you have a clear vision for where you want to go with your career?

2. Do you have a clear plan for how to achieve your goals?

4. Build Your Network

It is no surprise that networking came up often. We discussed it at length in this book. I generally credit networking more than anything else with my own success.

This advice is about taking time to network and connect with people in your company, in your industry, and in your field. It includes being willing to share best practices, challenges, and ask for help.

The vast majority of jobs are filled via relationships, which is true both inside and outside companies. It is often not what you know, but who you know that gets you an opportunity to work on that cool new project. And this is something that probably will not change in the foreseeable future, which is why I always recommend people start building their network as early as possible.

Some direct advice from my podcast guests on networking include:

- "Network, network, network." – Chicka Elloy

- "Expand your network." – Christopher McCormick

- "Be a connector." – Jeff Krautkramer

- "Network and stay connected on social media." – Lisa Lang

- "Get out and network." – Melissa Taylor

- "Build relationships with peers, clients, employees, etc." – Paul Chiames

- "Be patient and surround yourself with the best [people]." – Massimo Backus

- "Reach out to people and have conversations." – Phil Del Vecchio

- "Connect with people." – Jennifer Paylor

One interview that hammered this home for me and has stuck with me was an early interview with my good friend, Anthony Fryar, who left a consulting job to take on a completely new role as head of Learning & Development at AppDirect. To learn what it takes to run a great L&D team and create a "culture of learning," he talked to a bunch of L&D leaders at other companies (finding most of them via LinkedIn), and it helped him immensely.

I believe strongly in the power of networking, which is why I invest my own money in attending multiple conferences each year, and why I spend so much time engaging on LinkedIn.

That is also why I co-hosted a conference and later started an online community to keep connecting people in the virtual world.

Questions:

1. Are you spending time regularly building your network?

2. Who do you need to meet or want to start networking more with?

3. What actions can you take to start building a stronger network that can help your career?

3. Never Stop Learning

That should not be a surprise given that most people say, "Leaders are learners," and that most of my guests (and listeners) work in Learning and Development. We also discussed this back in Chapter 8 on investing in continuous learning.

That is not just about learning the latest trends in your industry. The most successful people I know take regular time for all kinds of learning.

Some advice we heard over the last two to three years includes:

- "Be a sponge, and don't assume anything." – Karlo Guevarra
- "Learn about the business." – Elena Ponce
- "Get to know as much about the business as you possibly can and . . . talk to people and learn from them." – Victoria Sevilla
- "Always be learning and work harder on yourself than you do on your job." – Kevin Delaney
- "Amp up your learning ability and try to learn something new every day." – Paul Rumsey
- "Find a mentor or coach who will speak truth and develop the ability to keep learning." – Julie Winkle Giulioni, author of *Help them Grow or Watch them Go*
- "If you want to teach people how to be good managers, go learn how to do that yourself." – Liz Wiseman, author of *Multipliers*
- "Be curious every day." – Gina Jeneroux
- "Never stop learning." – Teri Hart

And I love this advice from Lucretia Hall from SoftwareONE whose interview has been the most downloaded episode of all time (as of the time of this writing): "Surround yourself with good people and learn from them (every day)."

Finally, Whitney Johnson, author of the books *Build an A-Team* and *Disrupt Yourself,* suggested you "Focus on improving yourself before helping others," which is a hard thing to do for most people in L&D. You can hear more from her in the episode titled Why People Need to Disrupt Themselves.

I can tell you that spending lots of time and money on my learning and growth has allowed me to be a better resource to my clients and others around me.

Questions:

1. Are you consistently spending time on learning and development?

2. What resources do you use to learn, and when can you engage in learning?

3. Are you budgeting time and money regularly for learning and growth?

2. Listen

While learning is about growth, improvement, and perhaps understanding things about the business and trends that will help you do your job, listening is about making time and space to understand the needs of the people in your organization.

At the end of the day, we always have customers to serve and need to listen to their needs.

Some of the great advice we heard from guests on this topic include:

"Do more listening than talking." – Karlo Guevarra

"Grow big ears and a small mouth; absorb, ask questions, decide where to start." – Mindy Fox, Shutterfly

"Listen and keep the end in mind." – Yumna Ali

"Live among your people and be a cultural anthropologist." – Stacey Porter

"Be grounded in the science of human behavior and seek to understand people." – David Lusk

"Listen to your customer and ask questions to understand the true need." – Jill Coln

"Seek first to understand, then be understood." – Carolyn Kiel, quoting Dr. Stephen Covey from his book *Seven Habits of Highly Effective People*

"Be willing to take in information from sources you've never considered before." – Margaret Ann-Cole

"Connect and learn from other people." – Wendy Hanson

"Don't be afraid to ask the challenging, courageous questions." – Daniel Hallak

"Be exceedingly curious, ask questions, don't worry about looking informed." – Heather Hoerdemann

"Host listening sessions and find out what the challenges are." – Karyn Twaronite

And don't forget the importance of diversity in the people you listen to.

Are you getting input from different levels, different functions and groups, and other kinds of learners? And different backgrounds and generations as well.

In fact, Lindsey Pollak, who wrote the book *The Remix: How to Lead and Succeed in the Multigenerational Workplace*, advised we "get input from different generations when planning events or workshops." There are now many generations in the workforce, and we need to consider all of their wants and needs.

Questions:

1. Are you doing more listening than talking in meetings, your job, or your career?

2. Are you being exposed to a diversity of thought and perspectives?

3. Where do you need to listen and learn more?

1. Be Intentional and Own Your Career

This one should be obvious if you have been reading this book.

Most careers happen accidentally. Someone recommends a major or a course in college or a trade school, and we choose it because we don't have any better ideas (that's what I did). Or we take a job for money (or desperation), and several years later, find ourselves in that same field without ever really being intentional about what we are doing (that happened to me).

And there's nothing wrong with starting a career that way. We all have to start somewhere. Very few people are born knowing exactly what they want to do with their life, and even if they do, they often face unexpected challenges and have to make changes.

But at some point, we all have to take ownership of our careers. That means being intentional with where we want to go and taking full responsibility for our successes and failures. When you know where you want to go and have clarity on your vision, purpose, and goals, it becomes easier to make a plan, take action, and react to opportunities that come your way.

The best advice I can give you that will serve you throughout your career and as a foundation for all the other advice in this book is to take ownership of your career.

Questions:

1. Are you drifting or taking full ownership of your career?

2. Where do you need to take more responsibility in your career or life?

3. How can you be more intentional to achieve your goals?

Summary

There are many things we can do to accelerate our careers and achieve our goals. Choosing any of the above advice and following it will surely be helpful. If you can follow all of it, you will be a rockstar.

To summarize, it is important to . . .

- Take risks and approach things with a growth mindset
- Focus on your goals and avoid distractions
- Keep networking and building relationships
- Invest in yourself and your growth and never stop learning
- Be exceedingly curious and listen to colleagues and people around you
- Always take ownership and responsibility for your career and life

What advice is the most applicable and helpful for you?

I'd love to hear from you. Please be sure to share your best advice with me on social media. I'm always learning from others and updating as I go.

This appendix is also available as a separate report and course that you can share with your friends. For more career advice and resources and my report of the top five career mistakes that people make, head to our website: ownyourcareerownyourlife.com

BIBLIOGRAPHY

The following books have been mentioned, and I highly recommend all of them:

The Miracle Morning by Hal Elrod

The Miracle Equation by Hal Elrod

Never Eat Alone by Keith Ferrazzi

Think and Grow Rich by Napoleon Hill

Outwitting the Devil by Napoleon Hill

Sleep Smarter by Shawn Stevenson

The 10X Rule by Grant Cardone

You Must Write a Book by Honorée Corder

Freelance to Freedom by Vincent Pugliese

Get There Faster by Christine DiDonato

Your Best Year Ever by Michael Hyatt

Designing Your Life by Bill Burnett and Dave Evans

Mindset by Dr. Carol Dweck

Design Your Future by Dominick Quartuccio

The Coaching Habit by Michael Bungay Stanier

Measuring Up by Renee Vidor

Other books that have been very helpful to me along my journey (so far):

Awaken the Giant Within by Tony Robbins

15 Secrets Successful People Know about Time Management by Kevin Kruse

Live It by Jairek Robbins

The 4-Hour Workweek by Tim Ferriss

Man's Search for Meaning by Viktor Frankl

The Legacy Code by Armando Cruz

Essentialism by Greg McKeown

The Big Leap by Gay Hendricks

The Joy of Genius by Gay Hendricks

Tribe of Mentors by Tim Ferriss

10% Happier by Dan Harris

Multipliers by Liz Wiseman

The Miracle Morning for Couples by Lance and Brandy Salazar, Hal Elrod and Honorée Corder

Great Leaders Have No Rules by Kevin Kruse

Can't Hurt Me by David Goggins

Master the Key by Mike Flynn

ACKNOWLEDGMENTS

Thank you so much to everyone who inspired and helped me along my journey and throughout the process of writing this book. I am grateful to have such an extensive network of friends. There are a few people who stand out as being very influential and helpful along this journey:

First and foremost, my wife, Cortney for being my partner in life, my best friend, and more and more, my partner in business. Thank you for standing by my side through everything and helping me edit this book, making it 10x better than it was when I wrote it on my own.

Next, my children, Lucy and Teddy. You inspire me, entertain me, challenge me, and give me purpose. I love you so much.

Thank you to my parents – Larry, Shaune and Susan – for teaching me to love books. And to my brother, Spencer, for always making me laugh.

My journey has been heavily and positively influenced by friends and mentors like Vincent Pugliese, Jessica Lorimer, Hal Elrod, Honorée Corder, Gary Vaynerchuk, Larry Hagner, Reggie Shah, Nick Elkins, Dominick Quartuccio, Ken Carfagno, John VanderMeulen, Bennett Phillips, Jon Hodge, Jessica Parisi, Mike Kim, Chris Niemeyer, Tony Robbins, Jairek Robbins and so many more.

The idea for this book came to me like a lightning bolt during a conversation I had with Philip VanDusen right after hearing a great keynote speech by Jeff Goins at the Youpreneur Summit in London hosted by Chris Ducker. I'm grateful to all of them for influencing my ideas for this book.

Thank you to Honorée Corder for being my book mentor and coach and helping me plan out the purpose and marketing for this book; and for inspiring me to make a bigger impact on the world.

Thank you to Terry Stafford for your phenomenal editing skills and taking my writing and making it so much better.

Thank you to Rachel Richards (author of *Money Honey* and *Passive Income Aggressive Retirement*) for all your calls and advice while I was working on this book.

Thank you to my assistant and COO, Stephanie Hutchinson, for keeping me organized, helping me accelerate my business, and getting this book published and out into the world. You rock!

And so many other friends and mentors I've had along this journey (I wish I could name them all), THANK YOU!

QUICK FAVOR

Did you enjoy this book?

If you did, would you do me a quick favor and leave a review on Amazon? Reviews are the best way to help support authors and their books and it would be a great deal to me if you'd leave this book a review.

You can also grab bonus resources and connect with me by going to our website:

Ownyourcareerownyourlife.com

And if you want to get in touch with me, you can connect with me on social or email me at andy@andystorch.com

ABOUT THE AUTHOR

Andy Storch is a consultant, coach, author, speaker, facilitator, and connector. He is the host of two podcasts, including *The Talent Development Hot Seat* and *The Andy Storch Show*, and the founder and host of the Talent Development Think Tank Conference and Community.

In 2020, Andy wrote *Own Your Career Own Your Life* to help corporate employees stop drifting and take ownership of their careers, their lives, and their futures.

As a consultant and coach, Andy has worked with companies large and small all over the world. He has a BS from the University of Florida and an MBA from the University of Southern California's Marshall School of Business.

Most importantly, Andy is a husband, father, and friend who is on a mission to get the absolute most out of life and inspire others to do the same. He lives with his wife, Cortney, and their kids in sunny Orlando, Florida, USA.

Made in the USA
Monee, IL
19 December 2021